AI Readiness Assessment

Improve Your Organization's Odds of Succeeding with Artificial Intelligence

DR. SCOTT BURK

DATA—
DRIVEN
AI

www.technicspub.com/ai

Technics Publications
SEDONA, ARIZONA

115 Linda Vista
Sedona, AZ 86336 USA

https://www.TechnicsPub.com

Edited by Jamie Hoberman

Cover design by Lorena Molinari

First Printing 2024

Copyright © 2024 by Dr. Scott Burk

ISBN, print ed.	9781634623742
ISBN, Kindle ed.	9781634623988
ISBN, PDF ed.	9781634624930

The tricky thing about new technologies is that the vendors that sell and promote these technologies don't tell you about the hard part. The vendors go out of their way to not disclose the complexities that lie beneath the usage and the implementation of their new technologies.

It is incumbent on the buyer – the using organization – to discover and assess what these challenges are before making a commitment to new technologies.

Scott Burk's book fills in that most important missing gap. I recommend the book as a good starting point in determining your organization's readiness for adopting and committing to AI projects.

Bill Inmon

Denver, Colorado

Jackie, you are the best partner I could have ever imagined.
Bless you!

Preface

"Do you know the right questions to ask? Do you have a framework? When too many opinions are readily available, how do you know which ones to trust? My advice is to read a book."–The author

I am a believer in books. They provide something unique that we can't find in other media. For example, with a web search or a conversation with an AI chatbot, you lead with a narrow question or topic of interest. With a book, you can explore an open field and the author has spent part of their career with the subject and a lot of time researching it and thinking about it. The author knows the key ingredients you should be interested in and the ones to ensure you cover in your quest for knowledge.

That is the reason I like books. They provide an entire framework for the reader.

There are some great internet articles, even blogs. Experienced experts in the field do some. Some are done by authors without experience but have read many other blogs and articles and can now develop an audience because they are good with social media. Regardless of which type of author you get, these papers are narrow in their scope and coverage. There is no framework, no view across the landscape.

That is the reason I like books. The author writes from experience and a broad knowledge of the topic.

Today's internet is great because anyone can voice their opinion in a document or post. The internet is also terrible because anyone can voice their opinion in a document or post. Moreover, what is terrible is that I see someone spread something that is not correct, then someone else repeats it, and then it gets repeated. And the more it gets repeated, the more people consider it the truth. I can tell you, as a statistician, that if you sample from the wrong population, no matter how large a sample you take, you will never gain any knowledge of the right population. Ouch.

That is the reason I like books. The author should be able to defend and be accountable to their books.

I have been helping companies of all sizes in virtually every industry with data, analytics, and AI planning for years. I was an executive building a program inside the organization for many of those years. The difficulty is that I had to learn the hard way, through trial and error. There were books on techniques and technology but not on the organizational or business side of AI-driven decision-making. What are the right questions? What is the right organizational structure? Who are the right people, and what skills do I need most?

There were consultants and technology vendors, but they believed in a one-size-fits-all mentality. Their solution was the key to success. Not so much. I had to figure it out on my own.

Then, I was consulting as a data and AI architect for technology firms for many years. In that role, I too, suffered from seeing my company's product as the right solution for everyone. That was not my intention, but it was information bias. I was not knowledgeable of the broader solution space; I saw everything through the lens of our technology offerings.

Over the years, I began to see things more holistically and write about the broader picture and high-level questions. I became an independent consultant. Then, I could have open, non-biased conversations as an independent thinker. Moreover, I could address the real challenges which technology companies do not cover.

I realized that leaders needed an unbiased view, and that encouraged me to write a three-part book series to motivate leaders to get on board with AI-driven decision making and educate them in basic principles.

I wrote this book to help leaders figure out where they are in their readiness to be AI driven. What parts of the organization need to be considered? Please believe me, it is less about technology and more about basic business fundamentals. However, not any business fundamentals. The world is rapidly changing, and you need a special understanding of how to embrace the AI revolution.

I have seen many companies waste a lot of money and time attempting to do things with AI before they are ready. They should have paused to determine their abilities to carry out initiatives before launching them. And they needed to fill the gaps before they made major investments.

I concluded that I could offer more of a holistic approach to the process. This book solidifies and organizes that approach, much of what I have been doing successfully with organizations of all shapes and sizes over the last several years.

This book will be valuable for any reader interested in gaining insight into the application of AI for decision-making—for anyone who wants to avoid mistakes and expense by going through an inclusive study of their organization's ability to deliver upon its stated goals with AI.

Why do you need an AI readiness assessment?

The world is changing, and AI is changing with it. According to an IDC study:[1]

1. The overwhelming majority of survey respondents say that only about half of business decisions in their organization are made based on analytics.

2. 76% of organizations see the business landscape changing faster than in the past.

3. 93% of survey respondents report that they are not fully using the analytics skills of their employees.

4. 73% of organizations indicate analytics spend will outpace other software investments.

---

[1] Jan 2023 - IDC Survey Spotlight - Document number: # US50044723.

Why do you need an AI readiness assessment?

According to Gartner and VentureBeat, as many as 85% of analytics projects fail to deliver business outcomes.[2] Do you want to improve your odds of success? You must understand the factors essential to aligning your organization and preparing for the AI revolution.

We cannot take the "one size fits all" approach. Your assessment will be highly dependent on your history, industry, competition, and size, just to name a few important factors. This book is a guide and not a mandate on approaching your evaluation.

Philosophy #1 The purpose of good advice is not to tell you what to build. You must figure that out. The purpose of good advice is to show you how to build it better. And what matters.

Philosophy #2 It may not be easy, but it does not have to be overly complicated.

---

[2] Bean & Davenport, 2019, https://hbr.org/2019/02/companies-are-failing-in-their-efforts-to-become-data-driven.

About the Author

Dr. Scott Burk is the founder of It's All Analytics (itsallanalytics.com), where he advises companies on creating the optimal data, AI, and analytics architecture to maximize their objectives. He stays current by consulting, writing, and teaching. He is the author of six books on AI, data science, and analytics, including the It's All Analytics Series, the Executive Guide for AI and Analytics, and Practical Data Analytics for Innovation in Medicine. He currently teaches in the Master of Science in Data Science program at CUNY and has taught at Baylor and Texas A&M. He has developed curricula for several universities.

His experience is in solving difficult AI, statistical, and analytical problems at companies such as Dell, Texas Instruments, PayPal, eBay, Overstock.com, healthcare companies, energy companies, semiconductor and other manufacturing companies, startups, and many others across the globe. Scott has a bachelor's degree in biology and chemistry, a master's degree in finance, statistics, and data mining, and a PhD in statistics. Data has been the thread that has tied his professional experience together.

He now informs organizations on their readiness to deliver on data and analytics (AI) at It's All Analytics. He is always creating new content to make companies more effective and efficient by using data and analytics to improve their businesses. Scott resides in Central Texas.

Contents

i

Chapter 6: Operations and Structure_____ 111

Chapter 9: Data Assessment _____ **153**

Chapter 10: AI Technology Assessment _____ **169**

SECTION III—Project Selection, Remediation, and Kickoff 183

Chapter 11: Assignments Aggregated and Analyzed___ 185

Chapter 12: Executive Report and Presentation _____ 195

Chapter 13: Remediation and Projects Start _____ 201

Chapter 14: Parting Thoughts_____ 207

Index _____ 209

Introduction

"You either need to be a leader or a very fast follower - or you are going to be toast."

Clare Lunn

What happens to companies that do not adapt to new business environments? *They die.*

Death example #1

Business Death: Blockbuster, 2010

New Business Disruption: Internet Technology, Streaming and Changing Product Delivery

"Neither Redbox nor Netflix are even on the radar screen in terms of competition." - Blockbuster's CEO Jim Keyes, 2008

Blockbuster refused to see what was coming. They had invested so much in what had been a very profitable business model—video rental via brick-and-mortar storefronts. They had expanded aggressively and spent hundreds of millions of dollars in new stores across the

1

globe. At one time, a new location was opening every day. That caused them to be blind to what was taking place. They attempted to pivot at the very end, but it was far too late. The business was valued at $5.9B at its height, but in 2010, it filed Chapter 11 bankruptcy.

The company was too late to make the necessary changes in light of a changing business paradigm. The entire global market underwent a technological revolution, making new product delivery possible.

Death example #2

Business Death: Toys "R" Us, 2018

New Business Disruption: e-Commerce shift, Technology, Changing Product Delivery

"Thanks to each of you who shared your amazing journey to (and through) parenthood with us, and to every grandparent, aunt, uncle, brother, and sister who's built a couch-cushion rocket ship, made up a hero adventure, or invented something gooey. Promise us just this one thing: Don't ever grow up. Play on!" - Geoffrey, Toys "R" Us Mascot June 2018

Retail markets had been shifting to e-commerce for years, and Toys "R" Us was late in making the necessary changes to its sales and marketing model. It made attempts at an internal platform, but they had been in denial so long that they were late and could not deliver in a timely manner. **Denial happens often in business.** Leaders do not want to face their shortcomings and delay the obvious decision that needs to be made. In this case, it cost them the opportunity to shift into a new sales model. The internal platform could not be delivered on time. The effort was too slow. This delay forced the company to sign a 10-year contract with Amazon for exclusive rights to be its sole online vendor. However, the company claimed that Amazon breached the contract. The company sued Amazon. It was too late. The delay in understanding and responding cost the company its business.

There was a clear shift from brick-and-mortar retail to internet shopping, and many retailers were slow to adapt. The company was reluctant to move to unfamiliar technology, so it delayed its actions. Customers were changing their purchasing habits to more online purchases and fewer in-store purchases. Toys R Us was slow in adopting a new business model.

Death example #3

Business Death: Yahoo, 2016

New Business Disruption: Internet Retail Shift, Technology, Changing Product Delivery

Yahoo was a star. It could have easily bought Google in the late 1990s if it had seen the promise of internet search and its monetization potential. The price then, $1 to $2 million! The company said Google's Page Rank was not worth the expense. In 2002, Yahoo had a chance to buy Google for $5 billion. They backed out by stating the price was too high. In 2008, Microsoft proposed to acquire Yahoo for $45 billion. But the company rejected the offer. In 2016, they sold to Verizon for a mere $4.8 billion, while Google was valued at over $500 billion.

Yahoo discounted the power and value of search. They were slow to change in a shifting business environment. They stuck to a model of monetization via advertising *that had worked for them in the past*. They did not adapt to a changing market. Lack of innovation and change in a competitive world is a killer.

Death example #4

Business Death: Nokia, 2013

New Business Disruption: Market Shift from Hardware Functionality to Software apps

During a press conference in February 2016 to announce Microsoft's acquisition of Nokia, Nokia CEO Stephen Elop ended his speech saying, "We didn't do anything wrong, but somehow, we lost." He and the entire management team publicly wept.

Nokia was the first company to create a cellular network in the world. In the late 1990s and early 2000s, Nokia was the global leader in mobile phones. Over the years, the company invested heavily in research and development and invented its first smartphone in 1996.

Nokia failed to acknowledge the significance of phone software and underestimated the rapid transition to smartphones and the apps that drove the consumer market to move to them. In 2007, they earned more than 50% of all profits in the mobile phone industry! However, most of this market share was based on traditional cell phones, not smartphones. Nokia was slow to see the shift in the market. More importantly, they emphasized the hardware technology of the phone, not the software that drove smartphone apps. The smartphone market was rapidly changing.

In the same year, Nokia had over *50%* of the market share for cellular phones, the Apple iPhone was released. The iPhone sold 300K units in its first weekend. Nokia failed to recognize the shift of importance from hardware to software. *It cost them, big.* By 2013, Nokia had just *3%* of the global smartphone market, and in August of the same year, it sold its handset business to Microsoft for $7.2 billion.

Nokia did not adapt to a changing market. They continued to focus on their traditional strength, which was phone hardware. While they had developed a smartphone, they did not capitalize on what consumers loved about smartphones: the apps.

Why?

The reason for all these companies dying? They refused to adapt. It was too late to make the necessary changes in the business environment. Business environments were going through fundamental changes caused by the internet and related technology innovations. Artificial Intelligence (AI) will have just as significant an impact, possibly more. I will restate:

"AI will impact businesses as much or more than the internet did. Companies that will not embrace or are slow to embrace AI will die with all the companies we used to know that were slow to recognize the internet revolution."

Note that the internet revolution started in the late 1990s. Many of these companies held on, slowly bleeding out for almost 20 years. They may still be around if they had recognized changes caused by the internet and how it impacted so many business principles. However, they were too slow to adapt. They died. The AI revolution has started. Your organization will die if you do not recognize AI's impact, just as all these elite businesses did.

AI is the intelligence of machines or software, as opposed to the intelligence of humans or animals. AI is any methodology or technology that uses data to make better decisions. Examples include business intelligence, analytics, machine learning, data mining, and data science. See Burk and Miner 2020 for a survey of all these techniques and more.

Are you ready to compete in a new world powered by AI?

This is not a yes or no answer for most businesses. You might be prepared in some ways and deficient or absent in others. There is an old saying, *you don't know what you don't know.* However, *staying ignorant is not a winning business strategy.* Organizations must know how they stack up in their AI capabilities. That is why you need to take the time and energy to assess your current capabilities and what gaps exist that keep you from succeeding with AI.

What is an AI readiness assessment?

These are not merely technical abilities. On the contrary, leaders and managers must first get the culture and openness to change, bright people, an AI strategy that aligns with business plans, an organizational structure that works, and the right data and technology.

In the coming chapters, I will guide you through all these assessment dimensions and more. You must commit the organization and your leadership to be unapologetically honest in your assessment. If departments or teams attempt to sugarcoat reality, it will harm your ability to make the changes needed for success.

The basis for this book is simple. It is a tried-and-true set of principles, a method for any goal. It does not matter whether the goal is personal health, career success, or corporate success, this set of principles will work:

- **Principle 1** Where do you want to go? What is it you want to accomplish? Define the strategy or plan.

- **Principle 2** What will you need to do to get there? Define the tactics or methods.

- **Principle 3** Do you have everything you will need, or will you need to acquire certain things? Define the gaps.

- **Principle 4** Acquire the necessary tools and capabilities and execute the plan.

We will spend time with all four parts, but the majority will be on parts 2 and 3. Moreover, I will illustrate all the necessary dimensions for a successful AI program. Figure 1 shows a diagram of the four parts.

Figure 1: Four General Principles for Success

Importantly, we will not take the "one size fits all" approach. Your assessment will be highly dependent on your history, industry, competition, and size, just to name a few important factors. This book is a guide and not a mandate on how to approach your evaluation.

About the book

This book consists of 14 chapters and three major sections:

- Section I–The Essentials
- Section II–The Assessment
- Section III–Project Selection, Remediation, and Kickoff

The following is a high-level overview of the sections and how the book works.

Section I - The Essentials covers:

- The critical importance of adaptation.
- The importance of performing an assessment.
- Description of a process success, including four general principles
- The requirements of organizational commitment to an assessment.
- Evaluating whether your organization will have the discipline to perform an assessment.
- Factors that impact assessment work.
- The role of leadership in assessment.
- An overview of the assessment process.

The final chapter of this section is devoted to providing the reader with a high-level overview and appreciation of the assessment process.

Section II—The Assessment

Each of the eight chapters in this section include a description of the area and its importance to AI and analytics success. Each chapter includes material for the organization to work through and information that needs to be captured.

This information will be important to completing the final section. Here are the eight areas covered.

- Business Goals and Initiatives
- Leadership Assessment
- Culture Assessment
- Operations and Structure
- Industry and Market Assessment
- People Assessment
- Data Assessment
- AI Technology Assessment

These are the core areas for your organization to cover as individual assessments. At the end of each chapter, there will be an assessment questionnaire and a worksheet for your team to complete.

Figure 2 shows the 11 dimensions covered in this section.

Figure 2: Eleven Dimensions of an AI Readiness Assessment (ARA)

Section III–Project Selection, Remediation, and Kickoff

The book's final section analyzes the results across each of the eight-chapter assessments in Section II. This will provide you with a list of the business assessments you are most ready to implement and gaps to fill before starting your projects.

I also outline how you will be in a much better situation for future people, skills, data, and IT decisions because you have learned a great deal via the readiness assessment process.

This work will also provide an accelerated innovation environment for AI and analytics processes. It is like a flywheel effect. It takes much effort to get it started, but the momentum keeps moving it forward with ease.

We will also cover some future considerations for tweaking and optimizing the process for upcoming iterations.

A questionnaire or worksheet is included at the end of most chapters as dedicated assignments (homework). These will provide important questions and ratings for your leadership and staff to work through. The following is a list of important questions for you to consider:

- Have you read or heard about the impact AI is having on business and its future impact? How will certain industries be replaced with AI?

- Are you familiar with the evolution of AI chatbots and their impact on industry and employment changes? The replacement of humans in certain roles? Examples–ChatGPT, Google Bard, Hugging Face, Salesforce Einstein, and Microsoft Bing Chat.

- Have you identified how AI will impact your organization in the next two years? Next five years?

- Are your job descriptions changing to include more requirements for data and AI skills? Should they?

- Have you added any specific job roles specifically to address industry and market changes to be more of an AI-driven organization?

- How capable is your organization of adapting to changes in the market? Do you have an organization that readily adapts and is eager to learn new processes and technologies?

- Does your internal planning include the role AI will play in the future?

References

Burk, S., and Miner, G. D. (2020). *It's All Analytics! : the foundations of AI, big data, and data science landscape for professionals in healthcare, business, and government.* CRC Press.

SECTION I—The Essentials

One

Organizational Commitment

*"Having a vision for what you want is not enough.
Vision without execution is hallucination."*

Thomas A. Edison

It should be clear that your business must be prepared to make AI-driven decisions and take AI-driven actions. However, if you go in too quickly, you can waste a lot of time and money doing the wrong things before you are ready. This amounts to making bad investments and creating ill will within your organization. Therefore, you should do an AI readiness assessment before you dive in too far. This assessment will take you through an introspective process to determine your capabilities across the 11 dimensions that support AI success that we discussed in the previous chapter.

Will your organization have the discipline to do it?

It is easy to say yes, but this is an important question. Organizations always have several competing priorities. This is where leadership must be clear and allocate the organization's resources. *Will your organization make an assessment a top priority? Will the organization allow people the appropriate time to dedicate to it? What are the competing projects? What are the competing daily activities?*

I will guide you through the general assessment process. You need to personalize that process. *That is the plan.* That is the *"what"* needs to be done. I will offer help, but your team will need to figure out *"how"* to do it within your organization. That is the execution of the plan. As in most areas of life, *the more difficult part is not figuring out what should be done, but actually doing it.* Executing the plan.

To do this, you and your organization must be committed to executing the plan. The time it takes to perform the assessment varies based on several factors:

- **Culture.** A culture of trust will speed up the process. A culture of mistrust may hamper the entire process. A culture embracing learning and change will also speed up the process.

- **Size and structure of the organization.** The smaller and flatter the organization, the quicker it will go.

- **Department leadership.** If certain departments are more mature in AI-driven decision making, then they can act as a motivator to get the process completed so other departments can join in organizational success.

- **Industry and market forces.** Organizations that are more operational driven and less strategically minded will be slower to complete the process.

Obviously, there are other factors, but hopefully you get an idea of what is necessary. If you are dedicated, the process *should take a few weeks to a few months* to complete.

An important note for leadership

While some companies are not successfully executing their programs, there are companies that are very successful; the gaps are startling. Companies successfully competing on AI will clearly win out in their industries. In fact, according to **Deloitte**, the gaps between ROI Overperformers to Underperformers (Deloitte's terms) showed a **60 to 80 percent gap** that varied across industry.

Therefore, these AI-driven programs will only accelerate; organizations that successfully deliver these programs will survive and those that do not will most likely perish. The keys to success are the right leadership, accelerated adaptation, and execution. Leaders have two principal jobs:

1. developing (strategy) plans, and
2. executing those plans.

That's it.

What do you need to do? Create a plan. Make the plan reality and execute. Yes, leaders undertake many other jobs, but there are no more important jobs than strategy development and making that strategy happen. Embracing and preparing your business to be part of the AI revolution is strategy.

My intention is to be clear and simple:

- Your organization will need to be AI-driven in your decision making and actions, or you will not survive the long haul. Just as the internet has revolutionized the business world, AI will have just as large an impact.

- To be effective and efficient, you should view your capabilities to deliver results with data and perform an AI readiness assessment before you get too far.

- To perform this assessment, your organization will need a strong commitment.

The next chapter will provide an overview of the process and offer some suggestions.

Note: Smart CEOs and executive leadership get buy-in from the entire leadership and an internal buy-in across the management and key personnel. It is the old farmer preparing the soil. In fact, the whole assessment can be equated to the old farmer preparing the soil for planting.

Leader and management roles

Your organizational leadership must be the first to commit. The *CEO and CIO are the most important roles* to be on board in the executive suite, but in the end, you should have all your leadership and management convinced of the benefits of the assessment. They will have to lead the communication of the plan across the organization. They will have to execute the program. For small companies, this might be very simple. In larger companies, this will be more involved.

The heart of execution lies in three core systems:

1. systems of people,

2. systems of strategy, and

3. systems of operations.

Every organization uses these systems in one form or another. However, most organizations treat them as independent silos. This is a mistake. They are interconnected pieces of a larger system.

Important questions

Do your employees feel secure in their jobs? Do they feel they can openly express their opinions?

Do your employees trust one another? Can they speak candidly amongst one another, or must they hide thoughts and opinions?

Does your organization reward open, candid conversation or hidden agendas? Are leaders brought up through the internal ranks or hired from outside?

Do staff personnel trust their managers? Do managers trust their superiors? Does the organization trust the CEO and other executive leaders?

Are employees agile and quick to adapt to new technologies and new changes within the organization?

How capable is your organization of adapting to changes in the market? Do you have an organization that readily adapts and is eager to learn new processes and technologies?

Are employees typically positive toward change or reluctant to change?

Would you say your organization is hierarchical or flat? How does that affect the adoption of a new program or way of doing business?

Do you have any departments or leaders that could play a leveraging role to lead the larger organization in an AI assessment process?

Are most corporate initiatives self-guided or administered through a 3rd party?

Do you consider your organization proactive or reactive to industry and market changes?

How many leadership roles do you have in your organization? Do you have a hierarchical leadership or more of a flat leadership structure? How will this affect your ability to get leaders to buy into the idea of an assessment?

Do you have any highly respected leaders that you could call upon to lead the challenge? Would they sponsor the program?

What will you do when a manager balks and says the assessment is getting in the way of the urgent things that need to be done by her department?

References

Burk, S., and Miner, G. D. (2022). *The Executive's Guide to AI and Analytics: The Foundations of Execution and Success in the New World*, Productivity Press.

Two

An Overview of the Assessment Process

This chapter provides a high-level overview of the assessment process. It also offers some examples of how various businesses have conducted their assessment. It provides some lessons from others who have been through the process. We then take another view of the big picture from a different angle: The Six Foundations of the Success of AI Programs. We end this chapter with some important assignments.

We can formulate the AI readiness assessment as a project. A simplified design contains eight essential steps to complete. Figure 3 illustrates the project.

A numbering and sequence of these steps follows for quick reference:

1. Organizational Commitment
2. Project Team Structure
3. Top Level Education and Assessment Customization

4. Organizational Communication
5. Questionnaires and Worksheets Completed
6. Assignments Aggregated and Analyzed
7. Executive Report and Presentation
8. Remediation and Projects Start

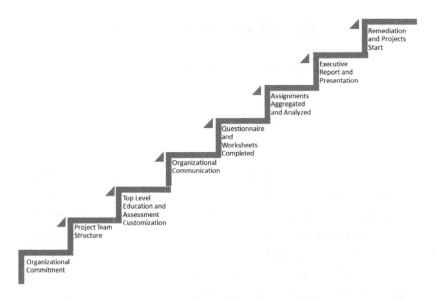

Figure 3: Simplified Business Readiness Assessment in Eight Steps

1. Organizational commitment

Organizational commitment was your assignment from the previous chapter. You should not advance any further in the project until you have established a dedicated commitment.

2. Project team structure

The project team structure may have many teams or as few as one. The oversight committee is the top-level team in your assessment process. It is the interface between all activities of the assessment process and the leadership team. As an overview, here is the structure of the assessment and teams:

1. **The Oversight Committee.** Highest level. Coordinating body. Interface with senior leadership.

2. **Business Initiatives Task Force.** This team will determine which AI projects to evaluate. See Chapter 3.

3. **Assessment Teams.** These teams actively review the organization's readiness capability across the seven dimensions of your organization. For small companies, it could be the same membership as the oversight committee. See Chapters 4 through 10.

4. **AI Implementation Teams.** Once the assessments are completed and the business initiatives to advance are determined, these teams execute the plans.

There are various team structures you can adopt for your oversight committee. There is no one-size-fits-all approach. Your oversight committee will depend on the size, industry, and organizational structure, among other factors. For larger companies, the Program Management Office (PMO) can help lead project management within an organization. Leadership must determine the best structure, but here are some examples of how various businesses have conducted their assessments.

In one small organization, the CEO, his executive assistant, and a consultant handled the entire process. Everyone had a different role. The CEO was the program sponsor, and his role was to illustrate the project's importance and get everyone on board by meeting with key stakeholders. The assistant coordinated schedules, meetings, and ancillary tasks. The consultant helped with communication, tailoring the questionnaires and the worksheets to the specific business and orchestrating the entire process. This worked very well for the business. Not only was the assessment very successful, but it also provided ancillary benefits. The CEO said the process brought him closer to his staff, and he learned a lot about the business because the conversations differed from those in his typical meetings. The entire process took less than a month.

An entire AI program was re-evaluated as part of a revamping at a Fortune 400 company. The imperative for this revamping was for the finance department to complete a cost-reduction project. It found that the AI program's accounting efforts and key performance indicators had been loosely formulated. The organization proposed a more rigorous method of determining the return on resources of AI projects. The CIO office revamped the entire AI program as part of the budget process and AI project planning. As part of that revamping, an AI readiness assessment process was implemented. The assessment also served as part of the annual budget process.

In a mid-sized semiconductor manufacturer with approximately 2,200 employees, senior leadership determined they wanted division leadership to work together to lead the effort. They did this to reinforce the company's traditionally strong cross functionality and their culture of working together. A committee of division directors did the project and selected the committee leader. The individual directors worked within their divisions to conduct their part of the assessment. Then, the committee aggregated the pieces and created the final report and presentation to senior leadership.

Note: Regardless of the team structure, trust is vital. People must trust the team leading the evaluation. People must be honest and candid during the evaluation. If you can find a consultant who can establish a rapport with staff, they may be seen as less threatening throughout the process. They can be extremely valuable. However, you should be careful in your selection process. You should have a consultant meet with several of your team members to make sure it is a mutual fit before hiring one. Also, if you hire one, pair them with a respected and trusted internal champion so the assessment will be open and honest.

---

3. Top-level education and assessment customization

The oversight committee must go through an educational process to understand the assessment components and the work to complete them. In some organizations, the program management office (PMO) assists with this process. In others, IT or HR may be helpful.

This educational process is critical for two reasons. First, everyone participating in the process must have faith and trust in the oversight committee. For the committee to be reputable, they must be fully knowledgeable about the overall process and its benefits.

Second, it will be necessary for the oversight committee to customize the evaluation project to the organization. This includes the communications, assignments, questionnaires, worksheets, and more. The following chapters will provide a strong foundation and methodology for the full assessment process. However, to be optimal, you must customize the provided materials and methodology to your environment.

There is not a one-size-fits-all that is universally optimum across all companies. The more effort you put into customizing the assessment, the better results you will get.

Once the project coordinator or project committee fully understands the assessment process and has customized it to fit their organization, they must communicate the plan with stakeholders in the broader organization.

---

4. Organizational communication

The organizational communication plan may be very simple for small organizations. It will be more complex for larger organizations. First, the oversight committee must work with its membership and management to understand the roles everyone within the organization will play in the evaluation. Next, the committee must create meaningful communication devices specific to those roles.

The objective here is not the assessment itself. The key objective is to communicate the importance of the assessment and how it will positively impact the organization. It is to establish rapport and commitment.

Stakeholders that are part of the process benefit in the following ways:

1. They help determine upcoming business goals and initiatives.

2. They learn about the broader organization and may expand their professional network.

3. They develop a better understanding of the organizational structure and culture.

4. They can develop a better understanding of their industry.

5. They may develop a better understanding of the organization's technology and data capabilities. They may influence future investments.

6. They have a unique learning opportunity and a chance to grow and potentially improve their professional position within the organization.

5. Questionnaires and worksheets completed

We will evaluate eight business characteristics or elements. Individual assessment teams carry out this work. Team membership may vary depending on the objective of the business element being assessed, or it could consist of the same members across the elements.

Each element will have its own questionnaires or worksheets to complete. Figure 4 shows this process.

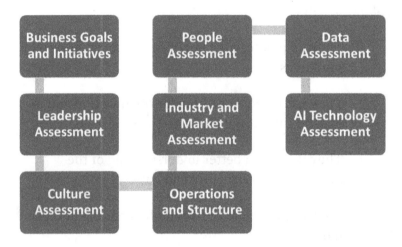

Figure 4: Eight business characteristics or elements to evaluate.

We cover each element in detail over the following eight chapters. The business initiatives task force will determine which AI projects to evaluate (Chapter 3). The assessment teams will be responsible for assignments in Chapters 4 through 10. Again, team membership may vary depending on the organization and the element assessed. They may also call upon other staff to help with the process. Yet, it is important that the oversight committee initially assign the most appropriate team members to complete the job. It is good to have some membership representation of the seven assessment teams on the oversight committee.

The following is a quick overview of the goals in the upcoming chapters.

Business goals and initiatives

The entire reason for performing an assessment is to determine your abilities to support your business goals. You may have existing business problems that you want to develop into a project. Or you may need help identifying opportunities to work on. In this Chapter, you will learn what some companies are doing to improve their business with AI.

I will provide you with a brief framework of AI maturity across industries. Given their maturity, I will outline some of the types of problems companies are addressing in their industries. This is insightful information because there is great reward in using lessons across industries. I have done this several times in my career. I will offer some real AI case study examples.

You will bring together your business initiatives task force. These are identified stakeholders and their representatives to work through a possible list of business initiatives you would like to accomplish in the near term, and you will select the top five to move forward into the assessment process.

Leadership assessment

Research across the five global industrial revolutions points out one common element of companies that were successful versus those that were not–top leadership was involved at every level of the organization and this leadership firmly focused on success. It begins with leadership.

There are stories about companies investing in amazing technology. However, technology is not the problem. **Over 93% of businesses report their people and processes are the problem, not technology.**[3]

Data-driven decision making, and the AI revolution are becoming the new norm. Adaptation is not an option; it is a necessity and that must be the message. The leadership team must drive the message through the entire organization. They must have a consistent voice. *Belief is important to outcome and leaders create the belief.*

The leadership assessment will consist of five steps carried out by the team:

1. Leadership Assessment Team Selection

2. Team Education

3. Brainstorming, Completing Questionnaires, Discussions, and Recording Materials

---

[3] https://hbr.org/2019/02/companies-are-failing-in-their-efforts-to-become-data-driven.

4. Scoring Leadership— Assessment and Gap Identification, Completing Mapping Tool

5. Share Findings with Oversight Committee for Aggregation

Culture assessment

Organizational culture is the shared values, customs, traditions, rituals, behaviors, and beliefs shared by the members of that organization.

We have discussed that organizations need a culture of openness to change and adapt to new market forces. Organizations need people who are willing and able to learn new things and ways of doing business. How rigid are the customs and behaviors within your organization? Are they entrenched and inflexible?

Do you have a culture of faith and confidence? Of trust? Do you have a culture of commitment?

Do you have a culture of loyalty and dependability? How open is the culture to new directions? How fast can the organization's culture shift if it needs to? These are important questions.

Cultural assessment is performed by leaders, stakeholders, and others identified to complete an assessment tool to rate the ability of the organization's culture to execute the top five business initiatives and determine gaps and weaknesses.

The culture assessment will consist of five steps carried out by the team:

1. Cultural Assessment Team Selection

2. Team Education

3. Brainstorming, Completing Questionnaires, Discussions, and Recording Materials

4. Scoring Culture–- Assessment and Gap Identification, Completing Mapping Tool

5. Share Findings with Oversight Committee for Aggregation

Operations and structure

The structure of your organization has an impact on your ability to execute with AI. Flat organizations are typically more nimble, agile, and quicker to adapt than hierarchical ones. Flat organizations are sometimes positively correlated with cultures of open communication and corporate allegiance than hierarchical organizations. Hierarchical organizations tend to be more political.

Operations also affect your ability to run your enterprise with AI methods. We will use operations in a broad sense. Is your business full of highly repeatable processes like manufacturing lines with rigorously specified inputs and outputs? Are the basic operations repetitive, and is there little creativity or new thought in meeting daily goals? Or are your operations highly dependent on creative input, such as producing new semiconductor designs for microcontrollers where each design is based upon customer input?

An evaluation tool performs the operations and structure assessments completed by identified stakeholders and their representatives. The assessment tool rates the ability of your organization to execute the top five business initiatives and determine gaps and weaknesses.

The operations and structure assessment will consist of five steps carried out by the team:

1. Operations and Structure Assessment Team Selection

2. Team Education

3. Brainstorming, Completing Questionnaires, Discussions, and Recording Materials

4. Scoring Operations and Structure— Assessment and Gap Identification, Completing Mapping Tool

5. Share Findings with Oversight Committee for Aggregation

Industry and market assessment

The industry in which you compete is highly correlated with the problems you face and what approaches might be used to solve those problems. At a high level, there are slowly changing industries with very consistent processes and market forces. Then, there are newer, highly evolving industries that require dynamic approaches. Some industries require a lot of human intervention and decision making, others do not.

Beyond the internal factors, external market forces also impact the way you approach problem solving for your business and impact the economics and levels of investment over time. All these factors affect your ability to respond with AI solutions.

The industry and market assessments are performed with an evaluation tool completed by identified stakeholders and their representatives. The assessment tool rates the ability of your organization to execute the top five business initiatives and determine gaps and weaknesses.

The industry and market assessment will consist of five steps carried out by the team:

1. Industry and Market Assessment Team Selection

2. Team Education

3. Brainstorming, Completing Questionnaires, Discussions, and Recording Materials

4. Scoring Industry and Market–- Assessment and Gap Identification, Completing Mapping Tool

5. Share Findings with Oversight Committee for Aggregation

People assessment

People impact all dimensions of a business, and we will expand upon this in the following major section, The Six Foundations for AI Success. For this assessment piece, we are focused on your current people's skills, acumen, and attitudes.

- Problem Design Skills–Translating a business problem into a technical construction.
- Business Communication Skills–Business Literacy
- Data Skills–Data Literacy
- Analytics Skills–Analytics Literacy
- IT Skills–Familiarity and competency with the organization's technology
- Business Acumen–- Ability to adapt and learn processes, interdependency, and interplay of the business.
- Attitude–Willingness to change, adapt, learn, and contribute. Desire to be a team player.

People assessment is performed by leaders, stakeholders, and others identified to complete an assessment tool to rate the ability of the organization's people to execute the top five business initiatives and determine gaps and weaknesses.

The people assessment will consist of five steps carried out by the team:

1. People Assessment Team Selection

2. Team Education

3. Brainstorming, Completing Questionnaires, Discussions, and Recording Materials

4. Scoring People–- Assessment and Gap Identification, Completing Mapping Tool

5. Share Findings with Oversight Committee for Aggregation

Data assessment

Data is the lifeblood of modern business. Data is everywhere. Data is in your mind, your experience, and your corporate systems. Data relevant to you even exists outside of your organization. You cannot make informed decisions without data. The data assessment is based upon several factors including:

- the organization's current data *capture* and storage
- the *consistency* and *quality* of that data
- the *availability* of that data to stakeholders
- the *security*, *governance,* and *compliance* with regulatory agencies
- the *sustainability* of the data streams

The data assessments are performed with an evaluation tool completed by leaders, managers, and identified stakeholders, especially IT and their representatives. The assessment tool rates the ability of the current data architecture and associated technology to execute the top five business initiatives and determine gaps and weaknesses.

The data assessment will consist of five steps carried out by the team:

1. Data Assessment Team Selection

2. Team Education

3. Brainstorming, Completing Questionnaires, Discussions, and Recording Materials

4. Scoring Data–– Assessment and Gap Identification, Completing Mapping Tool

5. Share Findings with Oversight Committee for Aggregation

AI technology assessment

AI technology refers to relative data transformation, translation, and modeling of data. The first type of AI could be any technology that enables enhanced human-assisted decision making (human in-the-loop decisioning). Examples here would be visual displays of data, business intelligence (BI), and third-party applications with embedded suggestions, graphics, or reports. It could be self-service reporting, or AI. It may be complex or as simple as spreadsheets.

The second type of AI technology is automated decision making or (human out of the loop) decision making. This is where actions are taken in response to machine learning or other AI models automatically either sending an action to be taken by another machine or representative.

AI technology assessments are performed with an evaluation tool completed by leaders, managers, and identified stakeholders, especially IT and their representatives. The assessment tool rates the ability of the current AI architecture and associated technology to execute the top five business initiatives and determine gaps and weaknesses.

The AI technology assessment will consist of five steps carried out by the team:

1. AI Technology Assessment Team Selection

2. Team Education

3. Brainstorming, Completing Questionnaires, Discussions, and Recording Materials

4. Scoring AI Technology— Assessment and Gap Identification, Completing Mapping Tool

5. Step 5 - Share Findings with Oversight Committee for Aggregation

Once we have concluded these first five steps of the eight-step process outlined in Figure 4, we conclude **Section II–The Assessment.**

We have three remaining steps, which appear in separate chapters and are part of **Section III, Project Selection and Kickoff,** as follows.

6. Assignments aggregated and analyzed

Once all the assessment elements have been collected, they must be combined to provide a final view of the organizational state of readiness for its AI-*powered business initiatives*. There will be a ranking of the five projects proposed in Chapter 3, Business Goals, and Initiatives. We will also identify strengths and weaknesses for each project.

The analysis will provide your organization with an understanding of your strengths and the initiatives you are most prepared to undertake. It will provide visibility into your readiness gaps and provide commentary on how you can use that information to improve your organization's readiness for the near and longer term. Furthermore, it can be beneficial in annual strategic planning and budgeting processes.

7. Executive report and presentation

Once all the assignments have been aggregated and analyzed, the project manager or leader of the oversight committee will assemble a small team to assemble an executive report for senior leadership. An executive presentation is also prepared as a summary of key findings and recommended actions.

The goals of the report and presentation are two-fold. One is to inform. The second is to secure senior leadership's commitment to move forward with the team's recommendations. These will include three AI-driven business initiatives to pursue along with any financial and other necessary resources the three teams will need.

After leadership has committed, formal communication with the entire organization occurs once the planning is complete. It will outline:

- The importance of the project to the future of the business.
- Recognition of the key contributors and participants.
- Findings of the project.
- Initiatives started as a result of the project.
- Corporate commitment to AI initiatives moving forward.

---

8. Remediation and projects start

Upon leadership's approval, work groups are formed, and the work starts. The oversight committee will form a work group for each AI project. These are called the *AI implementation teams*. They will carry the projects forward. Your organization may want to form an overarching AI committee or AI program office in the future.

Before we wrap up this chapter, let's take another big picture view of the foundations that support AI success from a slightly different angle. The assessment is more granular, but each dimension of the assessment can be mapped into one of the following foundations.

The six foundations for AI success

There are six foundations that form the success of your AI program. They are interrelated and nuanced. They are visually represented in Figure 5.

Simple descriptions of these foundations follow.

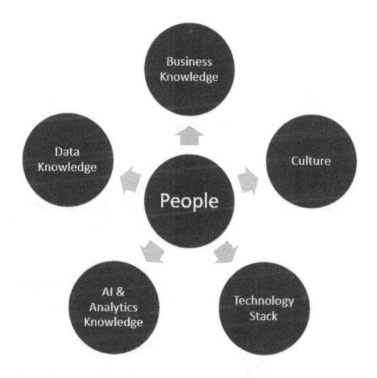

Figure 5: The Six Foundations of the Success of an AI Program

Business knowledge

Business knowledge describes the intimate and deep understanding of your business's operations and critical success factors. What factors contribute most to the success or failure of an enterprise? This includes intimate knowledge of your business's past, current, and future states. Which core capabilities led to organizational successes and lack of which capabilities led to organizational failures? What are the anticipated needs for success in the future?

Data knowledge

Data knowledge starts with the understanding that data reflects processes. So, in a way, data knowledge is an extension of business knowledge–the deep understanding of all business processes. Next comes the capture of data to represent the realities of the business–what your business is doing and what the results are. In between, the organizations must understand the types and structures of data and how it is collected, combined, cleansed, and used.

AI and analytics knowledge

Since data reflects process, the business can use that data to understand the interrelationships of inputs and outputs. How is *this* variable related to *that* business result? If I change this part of the process, what is the result? Based on history, what should I expect next year's demand to be? If I enable my organization with interactive visual dashboards, will they make better decisions? Can I build a machine learning model to predict what will happen if I manipulate all these inputs? Can I create "what-if" scenarios and analyze various trade-offs? Can it tell us the inputs that will optimize our margin?

These are the types of questions leaders can answer by combining these first three foundations.

One key component of these forms of knowledge is 'literacy.' Specifically, data and analytics literacy. AI program success requires many in the organization to have a deep understanding and literacy in these topics. Furthermore, you cannot build a culture without people speaking the same language. Therefore, everyone must have a basic business, data, and analytics literacy. This is an important example of how these six foundations are interdependent.

Technology stack

You need to design the right AI architectures to turn business, data, and analytics knowledge into results effectively and efficiently. You need to acquire and develop the right technologies.

Culture

Organizational culture is the shared values, customs, traditions, rituals, behaviors, and beliefs shared by the members of that organization. Culture has a major impact on your program's success as it influences the reception of knowledge and the use of that knowledge. A great Peter Drucker quote is, "Culture eats strategy for breakfast."

Therefore, leaders must understand their organization's culture.

People

The reason that 'People' is in the center of Figure 5 is that people influence everything. Who you hire, train, nurture, and promote influences everything. Your people are your organization.

In the next section, **The Assessment**, we conduct individual assessments by chapter. As we have seen, there are eight of these to be completed:

1. Business Goals and Initiatives
2. Leadership Assessment
3. Culture Assessment
4. Operations and Structure Assessment
5. Industry and Market Assessment
6. People Assessment
7. Data Assessment
8. AI Technology Assessment

At the end of each chapter, there will be an assignment, such as an evaluation, worksheet, or questionnaire for your assessment team to complete.

Chapter homework

You may decide to survey a larger group or only the oversight committee. Share these answers with the head of the oversight committee. Other important constituents that may serve the effort are a senior business leader who can be the project sponsor and a project manager. These individuals can use this information to craft education, assessment customization, and communication.

Please have key stakeholders answer the following questions and record the results:

How well does your organization embrace new corporate initiatives? Do they come in with an open mind and enthusiasm?

Which corporate initiatives were well received? Are there characteristics or factors that seem to improve employee buy-in or acceptance?

What was a highly successful corporate initiative? What contributed to its success?

What was a corporate initiative that failed? What contributed to the failure?

Please name three things the organization should have in place to improve the likelihood of success for your AI readiness assessment.

Next, form a business initiatives task Force for project identification. The next chapter covers the teams' responsibilities. This team will formulate a possible list of business initiatives. It will then select the top five from this list to move forward through the AI assessment process. (Chapters 4 to 10).

Note on Teams: Best practice is to use your project management office if you have one to coordinate the process. HR or IT is a good second choice. For each assessment team, you want business and IT representation.

Section II—The Assessment

THREE

Business Goals and Initiatives

"Begin with the end in mind."

Stephen Covey

The entire reason for performing an AI readiness assessment is to determine your abilities to support your business goals. You may have some business initiatives underway to support your business goals, have some in mind but not started, or be unsure what initiatives you should undertake. We will discuss ideas to get you there regardless of where you are. By the end of this chapter, you should have identified five initiatives.

NOTE: You do not have to develop your AI projects in-house. You do not even have to manage your AI operations in-house. First, you can use what I call **packaged analytics, which are analytics embedded inside an application** that your organization acquires to solve a business problem. Second, many platforms provide **AI services** like website optimization and other analytics. The benefits of using pre-packaged AI services are that they allow you to dip your toe in quickly, with few internal resources, and without a long-term commitment. At the same time, your organization's knowledge and culture will reap the benefits of AI thinking. *However, you should evaluate any AI project the same way. All AI projects under consideration should be run through an AI readiness assessment.*

We will use the five initiatives developed in this chapter in the following seven chapters to evaluate your organization's readiness and capacity to succeed with an AI-based approach.

Let us begin this chapter by quickly reviewing something we covered in the introduction, as it sets the stage for defining business goals and principles.

The basis for this book is simple. It is a tried-and-true set of principles, a method for any goal. We discussed those four principles in the introduction. Please review them if needed.

This chapter focuses on the first principle: Where do you want to go? What is it you want to accomplish? You may have attempted these business initiatives in the past but without success. They could be current initiatives that need to be revamped. Or they could be new initiatives that you have been considering.

Problems/opportunities/business case strategy

Getting your AI program started is often the most difficult part. A strong annual strategic planning process will facilitate this process. Using data to solve problems is a natural extension of the problem identification problem and attempting to solve them with intuition. To be clear, AI-driven decision-making does not have to supplant good business experience in the planning or solution phase. It may merely complement it. It depends on your organization and the problems you are attempting to solve.

However, a natural question is, how do we get started? Where can we apply AI within our organization? What business problems, issues, or opportunities can benefit from using these powerful tools? The short answer is that we can apply them to virtually every function of the organization. However, they may not be cost justified for every process. When getting started, you should realize you are facing some investment for the long term, so consider some expense part of the project investment and other expense as a training and learning investment.

According to a 2021 MIT Sloan Management Review (MIT 2021):

"The benefits of artificial intelligence go well beyond improved efficiency and decision-making. AI can also improve organizational effectiveness and strengthen teams and enterprise cultures.

Artificial intelligence can generate cultural as well as financial benefits for organizations. With AI systems in place, teams can perform tasks with more pride and confidence and collaborate more effectively: They can actually get stronger. These cultural benefits can penetrate the foundation of business operations, improving assumptions that drive organizational behaviors and ensuring the pursuit of smarter goals."

AI can reduce costs, improve execution speed, drive innovation, reduce or explain complexity, and change relationships with customers or suppliers. More specifically, AI can improve various business processes, enhance or enable products and services for customers, make better decisions, automate tasks, pursue new markets, or support other objectives.

Chapter homework

As mentioned in the last chapter, you will form a business initiatives task force. This team will determine which AI projects to evaluate. This is a team of selected business leaders and their representatives to work through a possible list of business initiatives, and you will select the top five projects from this list.

Your membership may include anyone. You may want to include a project manager from your project management office if you have one. A director or leader from the CIO's office might be the head of the business initiatives task force, or it may be a respected business leader in the organization. IT representation is always a good idea.

This chapter includes information on project ideas for your organization. At the end of the chapter is a template you can use for your organization or customize for your circumstances. Additionally, there is an example of a completed template with a fictional project.

First, don't overthink it!

We do not want you to overthink this initial assessment. The book's final section will discuss making the process more rigorous in selecting business initiatives. But, for your first assessment, you want to make it simple. You should go more with your recent history and your gut, and what you've been hearing from your team.

Obviously, I believe in using quantitative analyses and methods and in the future, you should consider such methods. However, I think you should use a less formal, less precise approach for this first pass.

Why? There are several reasons for this:

- **Simplicity.** Rather than boiling the ocean and spending a large investment in time and energy searching for a long list of ideas, you probably have a short list already in mind. If so, these ideas already have some knowledge behind them and some value to them.

- **Buy-in.** A critical need is getting everyone's support. The ideas already being discussed have a much better chance of buy-in than some new fad your industry is trying. You want to reach for the low-hanging fruit here and are much more likely to get support with a simple initiative than a complex one.

- **Emotion and urgency.** If you select a project to solve a burning business problem, you will likely gain acceptance enthusiastically and immediately.

- **Speed.** An assessment from the gut is more likely to move forward quickly and easily. And your first iteration is the most difficult and the most important. As we spoke about the flywheel, these assessments get easier over and over as you move forward.

- **Momentum.** It is always easier to carry forward an idea with some momentum rather than one from a cold start, a new one.

NOTE: Do not think that if you buy a prepackaged AI solution, you do not have to properly assess your internal abilities to plan and execute. Do not think that somehow the solution design will fulfill all your needs. It will not.

Projects

AI project definition is an important challenge. You need to translate the most important business challenges into problem statements that AI can address. There are many business challenges. However, thinking broadly and categorizing most of them is beneficial and not difficult. Typically, they fall into three categories:

1. Improve something.

   a. Improve Customer Service to Increase Revenue

      i. GOAL: Reduce customers going to the competition (preserve revenue)
      ii. GOAL: Reduce complaints (preserve revenue)
      iii. GOAL: Increase Upsell or Cross sell (increase revenue)

   b. Improve Catalog and Marketing Operations

      i. GOAL: Increase Product Listings (increase revenue)
      ii. GOAL: Improve Mail Recipient Targets (increase margin)
      iii. GOAL: Improve Quality of Customer Experience

2. Increase Efficiency

   a. Improve Product Quality to Decrease Cost

      i. GOAL: Reduce the Number of Returns (Reduce Costs)
      ii. GOAL: Reduce the Amount of Rework (Reduce Costs)

   b. Streamline Production

      i. GOAL: Cut Inspection Numbers with Sampling (Reduce Costs)

3. Reduce Risk and Uncertainty

   a. Reduce Revenue Risk

      i. GOAL: Reduce Fraudulent Payments
      ii. GOAL: Reduce Credit Default

   b. Reduce Legal Liability

      i. GOAL: Identify Insecure Contracts

Other problems and use cases exist, but more than 90 percent will fall into one of these three major categories.

Your industry likely has similar problems they want to solve. You can gather these via professional contacts, networking, and reading trade articles and business associations. Here is an example.

Plant nursery improves revenue and gains customers

A small nursery in Central Texas that had been in business for over 20 years determined it could benefit from an AI approach to customer contacts, marketing efforts, and customer support. It made this a strategic goal.

With some research, the company evaluated its options for the project. It determined three:

1. Develop this capability internally.

2. Subscribe to a Software-as-a Service (SaaS) customer resource management (CRM) system. It would have to configure the system and maintain the system.

3. Outsource the entire process as a service.

Leadership compared these options to the company's internal capabilities; skill level, learning capability and attitude, competing company priorities, business, operations, and IT resources. While the internal analysis was much more involved, the findings can be summarized as three options:

1. This option would provide the most tailored solution to what the company wanted to achieve. They would own it. It would require the company to hire outside IT consultants because it did not have capable internal staff to develop it.

2. This option would provide a model that works for other companies, possibly best in class. The company would have to adapt its needs to the platform's functionality. The platform was sustainable as long as the SaaS provider stayed in business or did not become too expensive. However, if they went out of business or grew too expensive, the nursery company would be left holding the bag. The nursery would also have staff configure, maintain, and run the system. Employees would gain analytics and data knowledge by managing the system.

3. This was a turnkey solution. It would require minimal effort from the company's employees, but it would not provide control, and it would provide the least opportunity for learning and ownership. It would leave the company very vulnerable to the solution provider's future.

The company selected option #2 and signed a three-year contract with the SaaS CRM provider with embedded AI capabilities. Leadership determined this was the middle ground. A great way to start its AI journey without a huge expense and long-term commitment.

Chapter Homework

You were assigned work in the last chapter to form a *Business Initiatives Task Force* of selected business leaders and their representatives. This team will work through a possible list of business initiatives that leaders, managers, and staff submit within the organization.

Your membership may include anyone. You may want to include a project manager from your project management office if you have one. A director or leader from the CIO's office might be the head of the task force, or it may be a respected business leader in the organization. IT representation is always a good idea.

At the end of the chapter, there are two important templates:

1. A blank template that you can use for your organization, or you can customize it for your circumstances.

2. A completed template. An example of a fictional project.

You may use these templates to gather ideas for potential AI-driven business initiatives. These will be turned into the Business Initiatives Task Force, who will select the top five from this list. These top five must be numbered 1 to 5. We will use these numbers to track them in the upcoming chapters and through the aggregation and analysis portion of the process. Let's revisit the process:

1. Educate your organization on the AI readiness program.

2. Encourage business leaders and staff to identify potential AI projects.

3. Have them complete the template provided or complete your customized version.

4. Submit their recommendation to the business initiatives task force.

5. The business initiatives task force selects the top five projects to move forward.

6. These projects will be evaluated over the course of the next seven chapters.

7. Evaluations will be aggregated and analyzed.

8. Leading initiatives will be identified.

9. Gaps will be identified.

10. An executive report that summarizes the results and proposed actions to be taken.

11. A corresponding executive presentation will be created.

12. Presentation and report conducted.

13. Remediation efforts and projects begin.

References

Burk, S., and Miner, G. D. (2023). *It's All Analytics–Part III, The Applications of AI, Analytics and Data Science,* Routledge

Larose, Daniel T; (2005), *Discovering Knowledge in Data: An Introduction to Data Mining,* John Wiley and Sons

Proposed AI Project

Worksheet Instructions

Please completely fill out the following form based on the following information:

Project Name / Submitter / Date–Name of idea, and person or group submitting the project along with date.

Business Initiative Supported–Please select from one of the following:

Revenue Enhancement

Market Share Growth

Cost Containment

Product / Service Quality

Customer Satisfaction

Other–**Define Specifically in the Additional Comments Section**

Estimated Benefits–Provide a quantitative measure of improvement, such as the $ or% increase over what period.

Summary Description–Brief description of the project.

Beneficiary–What department, group, or individual would benefit most?

Estimated Cost Items–Please provide a rough estimate of the cost areas and draft estimates. This will be explored deeper, but list obviously known items. For example:

Internal IT Resources and hours

Internal Department resources and hours

Consultant Services

Software or Contract Expenses

Recommended Project Sponsor and Team Members—List specific personnel or generic personnel requirements.

Risks/Constraints—List things that may hamper project success. For example, regulatory or governmental requirements. High-risk factors include personnel, technology, or other factors.

Known Gaps—List known skills, personnel, data, or systems gaps. This will be explored deeper, but list obviously-known items.

Additional Comments / Supplementary Information / Questions—Any additional information that may be useful in determining the viability and requirements of the project.

Proposed AI Project Worksheet *(TEMPLATE)*

Project Name Submitter / Date	
Business Initiative Supported	
Estimated Benefits	
Summary Description	
Beneficiary (primary)	

Estimated Cost Items	
Recommended Project Sponsor and Team Members	
Risks/Constraints	
Known Gaps	
Additional Comments / Supplementary Information / Questions	

Proposed AI Project Worksheet (EXAMPLE)

Project Name / Submitter / Date	AI-assisted Data Aggregation and Workflow, Scott Burk, 8/14/2024
Business Initiative Supported	Cost Containment Other–Employee Satisfaction and Growth
Estimated Benefits	Reduced overtime for entry and corrections would save $7,100 per month. Plus freeing up regular time. Employee satisfaction scores

	would improve for affected employees. Visual BI reporting and future AI forecasting methods. Admin time $.
Summary Description	There is a manual process of inputting data, verifying the data, handling handoffs, and communicating the WATS data into our corporate financial planning and reporting system. This is all manual input of data from existing data to two additional systems: Excel and the corporate mainframe. These workflows are manual and error prone. Certain parts of the process must be done in a serial fashion so that people are waiting on others to complete the process. They just wait until they receive an email or bug the person upstream that they are waiting for them. In the end, there are simple tabular reports produced which are often late after the accounting close cycle. The new process would link data and use AI-assisted verification so that the manual inputs are reduced, and accuracy is improved. This saves time and

	reduces errors. A workflow system would exist on top so that each person in the series responsible for verifying their data is automatically updated and everyone can see the status of all branch locations and steps in the process. The data is fed into a useful BI visual dashboard. This is executive and board quality information (reducing admin time for board meeting prep). The data is available in a relational database that can be used for other AI projects like forecasting.
Beneficiary (primary)	Branch Operations, Finance, and executive admin
Estimated Cost Items	Initial estimate for configuration is $25K + 4K per month (based on one estimate). Some internal training time and expense - $2K to 8K. Some internal IT resources.
Recommended Project Sponsor and Team Members	Adam West–Project Sponsor. Branch Operations managers. Julie Ferguson from IT and her designates. One person from HR (training and metrics).

Risks/Constraints	Vendor contracts–any legal issues? IT resources–time and knowledge/skill.
Known Gaps	Employees will need training. IT may be deficient on some technology. See Risks. There may be some employees in branches with long tenure who are resistant to change.
Additional Comments / Supplementary Information / Questions	Cost Containment–Labor and Overtime Hours Reduced Other–Employee Satisfaction and Growth. Employees are currently frustrated by the current process. It is very manual and labor intensive. It is not mind-expanding work. It is monotonous. Performing the work in a more systematic, computer-aided workflow would greatly improve morale and allow for higher-valued skills to be learned by employees. ROI Estimates–Year 1 Low $4,200, High $10,200. 2nd and subsequent years $37,200.

FOUR

Leadership Assessment

"Plans Are Worthless, But Planning Is Everything."

Dwight D. Eisenhower

The opening quote from Eisenhower is insightful. There is no doubt that Eisenhower was a great leader. He made this statement while he was Commanding General, European Theater of Operations (ETOUSA). He was referring to military plans. He meant that no matter what the plan was, something unexpected would arise to make it obsolete once the battle began. He knew no plan could be followed as originally designed. However, the planning process provided valuable insight and always beneficial lessons.

Hopefully, businesses are less chaotic and volatile than wars, but Eisenhower's quote remains true. There is much to gain from the planning process. Even if a prophet were to appear and provide a business strategy or course of action to leadership, something important would be missing. Much insight and intelligence is gained from the planning process itself:

1. Getting people in a room
2. Evaluating various strategies and plans
3. Respectfully discussing and arguing points and counterpoints
4. Understanding the strengths and weaknesses of each plan
5. Recording the results
6. Performing follow-up reviews and learning from them.

We spend too much time tending to the immediate and not enough time devoted to the important.

This is where leadership can make a difference. Leaders should decide what is immediate and what is important.

The immediate need is typically a short-term need that requires first-order thinking. What do you need to do for an immediate result? It is like playing chess by only thinking one move at a time.

Important things typically require a longer-term view. These actions should incorporate second-order thinking. Second-order thinking is like playing chess, contemplating your potential moves and how your opponent will react to these moves, and then considering your next set of moves. A good chess player does not focus on one move ahead; she thinks several moves ahead before she takes her next move.

Why leadership is important to AI project success

Leaders make the difference between success and failure in business and sports. A winning coach and his leadership team are the key to success. However, your leadership is likely distributed widely and deeply across your organization. Successful businesses cannot count on one individual leader to guide them to success. You need leaders everywhere and these leaders must be aligned.

Organizational alignment

The main goals of leadership are to determine the right course for the organization and then steer the organization on that course. This requires leaders to align the various parts of the organization toward this direction while considering independent needs and roles.

In 1989, Stephen R. Covey published the seminal book "The 7 Habits of Highly Effective People." The second habit was to "Begin with the End in Mind," and AI success is no different. Many organizations are keenly aware that AI is critical for a sustainable, resilient, competitive advantage when aligned with business strategy. At the same time, they often treat it haphazardly, not as part of the critical business infrastructure, nor treat data and analytic processes as a core strategic asset.

To use AI as a competitive advantage, business leaders must step back and articulate a clear strategic direction for their organization. This business strategy is more than mere hyperbole–leaders should include strategic goals, business objectives, and key results, often referred to as OKRs (Objectives and Key Results). Each of the OKRs may give rise to one or more business initiatives required to achieve those business objectives.

How would you rate your leadership's ability to communicate a clear and consistent message across the organization? Does this leadership align with the larger business, or do they take a 'lone dog' attitude? Do they have the ability to inspire the troops, lead successful projects, and implement change management?

One of the most famous works on change management was by John P. Kotter (Kotter, 1995). Kotter's book, "Leading Change," is widely considered one of the seminal works on change management. Although a detailed treatment of the Change Management process is beyond the scope of this work, Kotter identified an 8 Step Process for Leading Change (Kotter, 2014). Below are Kotter's 8 Steps for Leading Change Management initiatives:

1. Create a Sense of Urgency
2. Build a Guiding Coalition
3. Form a Strategic Vision and Initiatives
4. Enlist a Volunteer Army
5. Enable Action by Removing Barriers
6. Generate Short-Term Wins
7. Sustain Acceleration
8. Institute Change

When you begin any AI initiative within your business, keep Kotter's 8-Step Process at the forefront of your discussions. This is one of the most critical elements for ensuring the success of artificial intelligence projects.

Leaders are key in handling organizational change. Major changes in how the organization addresses decision making and takes action can have significant consequences for an organization–good and bad. You need strong leadership to guide your organization in this transition.

How successful have you been historically in guiding your business through major changes in your industry? New regulations? New competitors entering your market or location? An economic hit, nationally or locally? How would you assess your leadership on leading change management activities? These are important questions we will be answering in the assessment portion of this chapter.

Leadership assessment for your organization

Please review Chapter 2, "An Overview of the Assessment Process," where we discussed various team structures. The size, industry, and resources available to a company influence the team performing the assessment. In each of the following chapters, you will need a team dedicated to that part of the assessment.

NOTE: These teams may change in membership across the various parts of the assessment–leadership, culture, people, data, and more. It may be a few individuals or a full committee. A best practice is to assign a project manager who will be part of each team to provide consistency and continuity across the dimensions of the assessment. We speak in terms of a team, but that could be a team of one.

The following steps are laid out as individual meetings, but you may break these into as many meetings as you see fit. You should plan multiple meetings.

---

1. Team selection

You should select the team that will conduct the leadership readiness assessment. It should consist of a project manager or facilitator that will organize meetings and the work of the group. All leaders of any functional role should be included. Other leaders and staff may be included. NOTE: Leaders are not defined by title but by the role they play in the organization. Any staff member who influences project success may be a leader.

---

2. Team education

The goal of this meeting is to educate your team on the AI readiness assessment (ARA) process. Some of the items to discuss:

- The overall ARA process
- Information from this chapter, such as core leadership skills
- The five business initiatives, AI projects being evaluated
- Questions and Open Discussion
- Goals and Agenda for the Next Meeting

NOTE: It is important to have the five business initiatives. That is, AI projects named and numbered. You will use this numbering/order scheme consistently throughout the rest of the process. Additionally, you should have summaries of each project, including the functional departments and some of the key members contributing to the project.

3. Brainstorming and open exchange

The goal of this meeting is to educate your team on the AI readiness assessment (ARA) process. Some of the items to discuss are:

- Review and Opening Questions and Open Review Discussion
- Leadership and Organizational Behaviors and Capabilities Questionnaire
- Questions and Final Thoughts
- Goals and Agenda for the Next Meeting

NOTE: Some organizations meet to discuss the questionnaire and then assign it as homework to be reviewed as a team.

An assessment tool is offered in the following section, "Leadership and Organizational Behaviors and Capabilities Questionnaire."

4. Scoring assessment and gap identification

The goal of this meeting is to use the Leadership Readiness mapping tool to rate leaders' abilities to execute AI projects. Additionally, to identify potential failure points and gaps for each project. Meeting agenda:

- Open Review of Last Meeting Notes and Questions
- Complete the Leadership Readiness Mapping Tool
- Strengths and Weakness / Potential Failure Point Identification for each Project

You will find an example of a template and a fictional mockup with a discussion in the following section, "Scoring Leadership."

---

5. Share findings with oversight committee for aggregation

No meeting required. This is simply turning over the relevant materials to the oversight committee. This committee will be aggregating all functional parts of the ARA.

Questions for discussion

Gather your assessment team and any members of the leadership team and go through the following questions. Record the results.

Picture one or two **great** leaders in your organization in your mind. Without naming names, can you list three characteristics that make them great leaders? What do they do differently?

Picture one or two **lesser** leaders in your organization in your mind. Without naming names, can you list three characteristics that make them lesser leaders? What do they do differently?

How successful have you been historically in guiding your business through major changes in your industry? New regulations? New competitors entering your market or location? An economic hit, nationally or locally? How would you assess your leadership on leading change management activities?

Communication

How would employees rate overall **communication** within the organization?

a) Exceptional
b) Good
c) Okay
d) Poor

Which most accurately describes your organization?

a) Most leaders **are** personally talking with individual contributors within the organization on a daily basis.
b) Most leaders **are not** personally talking with individual contributors within the organization on a daily basis.

For leaders that **are** routinely communicating with rank-and-file staff, can you name who they are? What makes them different?

For leaders that **are not** routinely communicating with rank-and-file staff, can you name who they are? What makes them different?

Are leaders willing to have difficult conversations with employees? Would employees say they can be candid and open during these conversations?

How would you rate your cross-organization leadership on its ability to communicate a clear and consistent message?

Do leaders have the ability to inspire the troops and lead successful projects?

Independence and trust

Is the work leaders assign to staff normally performed independently by those staff? Or do leaders normally need to ride people to get the work done? Are there a lot of excuses made? What keeps assigned work from getting done?

If your team is assigned an AI project, is the leadership team ready to make sure the organization executes it and makes it operational?

Do employees feel empowered and supported by leaders and managers?

Do staff think they are on par with leaders or are leaders' part of an elite class?

Are leaders available for workers when they need them?

Would you classify the organization as a team sport or are leaders on another team?

Which best describes leadership practice–go get that done and do not bother me **OR** come with me if needed and let's get this done?

Do employees feel motivated to take action?

Trust and positive relations

Do leaders and managers reflect the company's values in their behaviors and interactions?

Do employees feel empowered and supported by leaders and managers?

How many employees would say that leadership 'walks the talk'?

a) less than 25%
b) between 25 and 50%
c) between 50 and 75%
d) more than 75%

Does leadership support initiatives initiated by employees?

Project Success. Which is more Accurate?

a) Leaders must be actively engaged for accurate and timely project success.

b) Leaders should be available to support projects when needed, otherwise leaders have confidence that the project will succeed.

c) Leaders should not be needed to support projects. They have their own work to be done and they hire people to complete projects independently?

What percent of employees say leaders are consistent and trustworthy across the organization?

a) less than 25%
b) between 25 and 50%
c) between 50 and 75%
d) more than 75%

Do you agree with this statement, "Leaders give subordinates complete freedom to solve problems on their own, but are available when help is required"?

Do leaders treat your employees the way you want them to treat your best customers?

Willingness to reward the learning experience

What percentage of employees say leaders are willing to take risks and avoid blaming individuals if projects fail?

a) less than 25%
b) between 25 and 50%
c) between 50 and 75%
d) more than 75%

What percent of employees say your organization is innovative given its industry and market?

a) less than 25%
b) between 25 and 50%
c) between 50 and 75%
d) more than 75%

What percent of employees say your organization learns from its mistakes?

a) less than 25%
b) between 25 and 50%
c) between 50 and 75%
d) more than 75%

How do you handle failure and setbacks?

Is leadership consistent in the way it treats setbacks? Or does it vary widely across the organization? Are there leaders people feel are willing to accept setbacks as a learning experience and others that want to punish setbacks?

Would you say leaders are comfortable taking risks? Does your organization learn from, and then forget mistakes?

Does leadership reward success and punish failure?

Alignment and collaboration

What percent of employees say different departments work well together when necessary? If projects require cross-departmental effort, do the departments work well together or retreat to their turf?

a) less than 25%
b) between 25 and 50%
c) between 50 and 75%
d) more than 75%

What percent of employees say leadership is clear about their department's role in the overall strategy/plan for the organization?

a) less than 25%
b) between 25 and 50%
c) between 50 and 75%
d) more than 75%

What percent of employees say there is leadership prejudice? That is, is there favoring of certain departments? Toward certain individuals?

a) less than 25%
b) between 25 and 50%
c) between 50 and 75%
d) more than 75%

Does leadership support cross-department career growth, meaning if an employee wanted to take on a new role in another department, would the current leaders support that move?

Do leaders across departments often communicate with one another? Do they work well together?

Do rank and file staff know how their work ties into corporate strategy or the CEO's priorities?

Does this leadership align with the larger business, or do they take a 'lone dog' attitude?

Commitment

What percentage of employees say that once leadership commits to a project, it provides all the necessary resources to complete it?

a) less than 25%
b) between 25 and 50%
c) between 50 and 75%
d) more than 75%

What percent of employees say that leadership is constantly changing priorities?

a) less than 25%
b) between 25 and 50%
c) between 50 and 75%
d) more than 75%

Have you seen leadership make personal sacrifices to save a project or effort that is at risk of failure?

Do you think leaders are loyal to the company? Very loyal? Not at all?

Would you say employees are passionate about their work or would they say they work for a paycheck?

Would you say leaders are passionate about their work or would they say they work for a paycheck?

Does leadership require as much personal sacrifice from themselves as they do the rest of the organization?

Scoring assessment and gap identification

This is Step 4 (summarized in the previous overview section). In this step of the assessment, you will have an open discussion with your team and come up with your capability rating for the five projects you have selected in Chapter 3, "Business Goals and Initiatives."

Figure 6 shows a blank template for you to use. Your five business goals appear down the left side. Across the top are four areas of leadership competency. You will fill in the 20 cells with a rating from 1 to 10 with the lowest rating being a 1 which means you are not at all capable with this competency for this initiative, up to a high rating of 10 which means you are fully capable and have no barriers or gaps in this competency to complete the initiative. You will provide a copy of your completed mapping results to the oversight committee.

Next, we illustrate the process with an example.

Rate Each Cell 1 to 10 where:
Rating of 1 – Not at All Capable
Rating of 10 – Fully Capable, Zero Gaps

Business Goal	Trust and Positive Relations	Willingness to Take Chances and Not Blame Failures, Reward Learning	Alignment and Collaboration	Commitment
1				
2				
3				
4				
5				

Figure 6: Scoring Leadership - Readiness Mapping Tool Template

Figure 7 contains five mock business goals we want to evaluate as potential AI projects over the next year.

1. Reduce manufacturing cost by 5%

2. Cut expense statement processing time to less than five days with 95% accuracy

3. Improve customer retention by 7%

4. Reduce customer service call times by 10%

5. Improve customer satisfaction score by 6 points

These are ordered down the left side (again, you should always be consistent in your ordering, as at the end of the assessment we will aggregate everything). Across the top are four areas of leadership competency.

The team has spent time and energy discussing each rating for each cell in this worksheet. We need an open discussion of why they think the initiative would likely be successful or not. The team carefully identified strengths and weaknesses that would contribute to the likelihood of each

AI project being completed. A scribe has captured the key points of the discussion. As a result, the team also determined the 20 scores and entered them in the worksheet.

We can see the team rated the strength of executing project #1 as 6 for trust and positive relations. For project #2, they rated the strength of executing project #2 as 7 for trust and positive relations, etc. Looking across the various initiatives, it appears that #3 and #5 rated much higher.

1 Reduce Manufacturing cost by 5%
2 Cut expense statement processing time to less than 5 days with 95% accuracy
3 Improve Customer Retention by 7%
4 Reduce customer service call times by 10%
5 Improve Customer Satisfaction Score by 6 points

Business Goal	Trust and Positive Relations	Willingness to Take Chances and Not Blame Failures, Reward Learning	Alignment and Collaboration	Commitment
1	6	6	6	7
2	7	8	8	6
3	8	9	9	10
4	8	8	9	6
5	8	9	9	10

Figure 7: Scoring Leadership–Readiness Mapping Tool Example

Identification of strengths and weakness / potential failure points

The last part of the assessment to be passed onto the oversight committee will be a list of strengths and weaknesses that can impact the likelihood of success for the initiative. We noted that projects #3 and #5 had much higher scores for likely project success than project #1.

Why? Based on the team's input, the scribe has documented the reasons for these differences. We summarize these below as strengths and weaknesses.

In the open discussion for project #3 (Improve Customer Retention by 7%), we learn that the marketing department will play a key role in this project. Marketing is led by Susan Pinker (pseudonym), and she is a tremendous leader who is well respected in the organization. She has an impeccable record of success. She also has a way of getting cross-functional support and alignment. Project #1 (Reduce Manufacturing cost by 5%) is a complicated project that requires IT, engineering, and manufacturing to work together. There has been some history that demonstrates the difficulty in getting these leaders aligned.

Along with the scores, the leadership assessment team passed on the top three success contributors and antagonists.

An example that scored lower than most, "#1 Reduce Manufacturing Cost by 5%."s

Top Three Contributors for Success - #1 Reduce Manufacturing Cost by 5%

1. The engineering team has invested heavily in training. Statistical Process Control and Lean Manufacturing.

2. Three engineering interns would be available to help with the project this summer.

3. Manufacturing received a budget for process prototyping. This could bootstrap the project, and

top leadership would love to use that budget for this project. The result would be significant motivation and momentum.

Top Three Antagonists Against Success - #1 Reduce Manufacturing cost by 5%.

1. The new ERP system is scheduled, and IT will not have much bandwidth. We can contract out some of the effort, but there is always a need for internal subject matter expertise.

2. Last year's major retooling project showed that IT and manufacturing do not always work well together.

3. Ben Jefferson just retired, and Susan Mathison will be on a sabbatical for four months this year.

Another example that scored higher than most, "#3 Improve Customer Retention by 7%.".

Top Three Contributors for Success - #3 Improve Customer Retention by 7%

1. Susan Pinker has been advocating for this. She will be enthusiastic and will drive this home. She has a track record of getting it done.

2. Redundant, but Susan got four departments to work together on the Evenflo project—she might have been the only one that could do that. This project should go much more smoothly.

3. There is not a great deal of work outside one department, so that will facilitate and expedite things.

Top Three Antagonists Against Success - #3 Improve Customer Retention by 7%

1. Success is very dependent on one individual. While we think there is little risk of something happening to her, it is always a chance.

2. There could be unforeseen external forces that may affect the ability to execute.

3. We plan to hire several new people this year. Will they integrate well and succeed?

Next, we address the contribution of culture to AI project success.

References

Bahcall, Safi (2019) *Loonshots: How to Nurture the Crazy Ideas That Win Wars, Cure Diseases, and Transform Industries* St. Martin's Press.

Bean and Davenport, 2019; Companies are failing in their efforts to become data-driven; https://hbr.org/2019/02/companies-are-failing-in-their-efforts-to-become-data-driven.

Lockwood, T., and Papke, E. (2017). *Innovation by design: How Any Organization Can Leverage Design Thinking to*

Produce Change, Drive New Ideas, and Deliver Meaningful Solutions. Red Wheel/Weiser.

Kotter, J. P. (1995). Leading change: Why transformation efforts fail (Vol. 73). *New York: Harvard Business School Publication Corp*

Kotter, John P. Accelerate: Building Strategic Agility for a Faster-Moving World. Harvard Business Review Press, 2014.

FIVE

Culture Assessment

"A company's culture is the foundation for future innovation."

Brian Chesky, Co-founder, and CEO of Airbnb

Ask a dozen people, "What is culture?" and you will get two dozen answers. It is hard to define. Some might say, I can't tell you what it is, but I know it when I see it. That is not helpful.

The best definition we can use is the one we discussed in Chapter 2, "Organizational culture is the shared values, customs, traditions, rituals, behaviors, and beliefs shared by the members of that organization."

Culture has been responsible for many corporate successes like Southwest Airlines, Patagonia, and HubSpot. And there are many, many more cases where corporate culture led to corporate demise.

Why culture is important to AI project success

An AI mindset is a paradigm shift. When you change how you approach your business problems, you must consider your culture. Consider the impact on your people, their values, customs, traditions, rituals, behaviors, and beliefs shared by the members of that organization. If you fail to do this, your organization will suffer.

The likelihood of your AI projects failing is higher if you do not consider the cultural impact of these efforts. And worst yet, you may misidentify the reason for that failure. You may attribute it to poor leadership, poor management, lack of budget or technical skills, or some other reason when, in fact, it was due to not accounting for and addressing your culture.

Foundations of the new AI and analytics culture

How does a business ensure that it gets the most from the wealth of data?

- Leaders and management must think analytically and
- Leadership must create a culture where AI and AI specialists will thrive.

Your understanding of your culture is key to determining your organization's ability to complete successful AI projects.

Culture's role in AI projects

Culture impacts all facets of your organization. It has less impact when it is business as usual. It has *a significant impact* when trying to change how you approach decision making and operations.

The degree of these forces will vary depending on the projects you select and your unique circumstances. The following example illustrates some positive cultural characteristics and some gaps when I was leading a project for Texas Instruments.

Culture lessons from the AI front

In the mid-1990s, Texas Instruments (TI) was in the middle of a war with Dell and Toshiba. The company had invested $1B (1995 $s) in plant, equipment, distribution centers, and personnel. The plant in Central Texas was nearly a million square feet. It was the headquarters for personal productivity products, meaning it was the only TI business that focused on end user or consumer products.

TI's strategy for this business was to design and develop the fastest, smartest, best-engineered notebooks in the market. TI was an engineering company. That was its culture. Engineers led the company and have led it since its founding. It was the way they thought about everything. They considered an engineering approach optimal in every function. It defined successful strategies in the semiconductor, defense, and other lines of business, so why shouldn't it work for the consumer arm of the business, including notebook computers?

As their key product differentiator, TI was betting on early product introduction and performance. Therefore, it was paramount that new products be rolled out well ahead of the competition. A new product leader in the market had a substantial advantage over the competition. This allowed that leader to gain substantial profit margins that fueled their flywheel. More profit leads to more innovation, leads to more sales, and leads to more profit. Being late to market was a killer—you could not recoup your investment. You were lucky to break even if you were in the middle of the pack.

There are many things that have to come together for a new line of notebooks to be brought to market—design, engineering, manufacturing, marketing, finance, customer support, logistics, channel partners, and more. So, there were many points of potential failure, and the business had more control over some of them than others.

Target business problems

- We have several potential product lines. Which should we invest in?
- For financial planning, how can we model profitability, cash flow, and accounting budgets?
- For a given product line, where will we need to shift resources? How should we plan?

- For marketing and sales, how should we adjust resources?
- What are the probabilities of delays and how does this affect projected profitability?
- What are the probabilities of delays and how does this affect cash flow?
- What are the probabilities of delays and how does this affect supply logistics?
- What are the probabilities of delays and how does this affect our partner relationships?

Before the AI solution

The finance department was responsible for working with engineering, manufacturing, logistics, and sales and marketing. It had models in spreadsheets that addressed many of the targets. However, these models were not robust. Some of the issues with their models:

- All models were static, single cell spreadsheet inputs.
- No modeling for upside or downside risk.
- No ability to do scenario analysis.
- No capability to determine key influences of delays, profit margins, or any financial metrics.
- No forecasting capability.

Potential of an AI solution

Being a student of AI and simulation, I understood we could quickly adapt our static spreadsheet models into dynamic predictive modeling with Monte Carlo simulation. With a few weeks of conversion and enhancement of the models and a few weeks of education, we could radically shift our decision-making process. The only additional part that needed to be added beyond the conversion was to add some forecasting capability.

Moreover, I did not use any sophisticated technical tools. I knew the team was very comfortable and capable of using Microsoft Excel. I kept the Excel backbone and created the AI simulation and forecasting in the background of the spreadsheets.

We were able to reverse all the negatives mentioned above to:

- All inputs were statistical distributions based on subject matter expertise.
- We could model for upside or downside risk.
- We could do scenario analysis.
- We could determine key influences of delays, profit margins, and other financial metrics.
- We could forecast all the key metrics.

We then could provide all the key stakeholders with the information they needed to optimize their decisions, alter their resource allocations, and feel confident about the results.

Cultural strengths that led to project deliverable success

What were some of the key cultural ingredients of the project's success? The following were the key ingredients for the project, and they offer a solid foundation for any team wanting to get results with AI:

- A tradition of being flexible.
- An openness to change and being adaptable.
- A culture that embraced learning.
- A culture of continual improvement and growth.
- Exhibiting mutual respect for one another.
- Team focus. If the team wins, we all win.
- Forward and future looking. Valuing technology and new methods.
- Willingness to risk failure.
- A culture of innovation.

We just covered several of the cultural strengths that led to project success. I feel the project deliverables were a success. This means the technical details were sound, and the models ran as specified.

There was a great improvement in overall information quality. Everyone agreed and acknowledged the information was extremely useful and had great operational benefit.

However, the business unit had mixed results. Some product lines improved, but some significant delays cost a great deal of potential profit margin. Models cannot solve every problem. We had supply and other issues.

NOTE: You should outline specific criteria for project success. These success criteria should only account for what the project is designed to control. If you reach these goals, your project should be deemed a success. Regardless, you should always do a business review after the project and document any lessons you learned.

Culture assessment for your organization

As in the previous chapter, the following steps are laid out as individual meetings, but you may break these into as many meetings as you see fit. You should plan multiple meetings.

---

1. Team selection

You should select the team that will conduct the culture readiness assessment. It should consist of a project manager or facilitator who will organize meetings and the group's work. In addition, a cross-functional membership of personnel that may have any unbiased and meaningful contribution assesses cultural readiness to contribute to project success and identifies factors that may impede that success.

---

2. Team education

This meeting aims to educate your team on the AI readiness assessment (ARA) process. Items to discuss are:

- The overall ARA process·
- Information from this chapter, such as core culture skills

- The five projects to evaluate
- Questions and open discussion
- Goals and agenda for the next meeting

NOTE: It is important to have the five projects named and numbered. You will use this numbering/order scheme consistently throughout the rest of the process. Additionally, you should have summaries of each project, including the functional departments and some of the key members contributing to the project.

---

3. Brainstorming and open exchange

This meeting aims to educate your team on the AI readiness assessment (ARA) process. Some of the items to discuss are:

- Review and opening questions and open review discussion
- Culture and its impact questionnaire
- Questions and final thoughts
- Goals and agenda for the next meeting

NOTE: As before, some organizations meet to discuss the questionnaire, assign it as homework, and then review it as a team.

An assessment tool is offered in the following section, "Culture and Its Impact Questionnaire."

4. Scoring culture - assessment and gap identification

The goal of this meeting is to use the Culture Readiness mapping tool to rate the organizations' ability to execute AI projects. Additionally, to identify potential failure points and gaps for each project. Meeting agenda:

- Open review of last meeting notes and questions
- Complete the culture readiness mapping tool
- Strengths and weakness / potential failure point identification for each project

You will find an example of a Readiness Mapping Tool template in the following section, "Scoring Culture."

5. Share findings with oversight committee for aggregation

Instead of a meeting, this is just turning over the relevant materials to the oversight committee. This committee will be aggregating all functional parts of the ARA.

Questions for discussion

Gather your assessment team and any members of the leadership team and go through the following questions. Record the results.

What do employees like most about the organization's culture?

What are your culture's greatest strengths? Its greatest weaknesses?

If asked, what would employees want to change about the organization's culture?

What will you find your people doing when no one is watching?

What is the best single word that describes your culture (e.g., daring, honest, bright, sincere, loyal)?

Describe in a single word, what is your greatest cultural strength?

Describe in a single word, what is your greatest cultural weakness?

Flexibility / adaptability and ability to change

How has your organization's culture changed as it has grown? Has the culture strengthened or weakened with growth?

Do you have an agile, adaptive culture?

Would your people like change or prefer the business and market environment to stay the same?

Can you name a time when the organization overcame a significant challenge? What were the key characteristics that made this possible? Who was involved? What behaviors did they exhibit to lead to success?

If your organization outsourced a function such as payroll, would your organization reassign the people affected or would they be laid off?

How did your organization react to COVID? How would you rate this response? Did you learn from the experience?

If there was another pandemic, do you feel confident your organization would respond as well as your competition?

How open is the culture to new directions? How fast can the organization shift its culture if it needs to?

Community, team strength, and innovation

Do your people support one another as a tight-knit supportive culture?

Do your people like working together?

Are your people patient with one another?

Do you people care about each other?

Can you name specific examples where your culture had a challenging task and came together to accomplish it?

Can you name a time when your organization faced a crisis and your people banded together and came through it as a team?

Is there a basic code of human decency in your organization? Is there a golden rule for employees to treat each other how they want to be treated? Or is it a high-pressure environment where the norm is to advance oneself for the sake of others?

What percent of employees say different departments work well together when necessary?

a) less than 25%
b) between 25 and 50%
c) between 50 and 75%
d) more than 75%

What percent of employees say there is a culture of departmental prejudice pitting departments against one another?

a) less than 25%
b) between 25 and 50%
c) between 50 and 75%
d) more than 75%

What percentage of employees say there is a culture of individual prejudice pitting people against one another?

a) less than 25%
b) between 25 and 50%
c) between 50 and 75%
d) more than 75%

Are people communicating with each other at work? Do communication gaps cause problems?

Loyalty, commitment, and risk taking

Do your employees have a strong sense of self-interest? Company interest? Or a balance?

Do your people want to come to work? Is there a sense of satisfaction and fulfillment at work?

Are your best people referring their friends to work for your organization? Are they bringing in new hire candidates?

Do people trust the leadership of the company?

Would your employees say the leadership is transparent? Is leadership willing to share details with front-line employees?

Is there alignment between the service you provide and the organization's values?

How often do employees say, "That is not my job" or "That is not in my job description"?

What is your employee turnover rate? Is it consistent year over year or are there spikes? Does it occur in a certain chain of command in your organization?

Do you actively work on getting rid of employees who do not fit your culture? Your mission? Your purpose? Do you make a dedicated effort to weed out the wrong people while working on retaining the right people?

Is your organization more fact driven or more emotionally driven?

Do you have a culture of commitment?

Do you have a culture of loyalty and dependability?

Learning, improvement, and innovation

How rigid are the customs and behaviors within your organization? Are they entrenched and inflexible?

Does the company offer internal training? Tuition reimbursement? Support for conferences, seminars, or workshops?

Is your organization behind the competition in innovation? Ahead?

Do people ask, "How can we do this better?"

Does management and leadership support ideas initiated by staff?

Do you have specific programs or budgets to improve your culture or employee retention?

Would you consider your culture innovative?

Do you feel the work environment encourages innovation and creativity?

Do employees feel safe and respected when sharing their ideas and opinions?

Do you have a culture of discovery where people are open to new ways of doing things? Are people open-minded?

Scoring culture - assessment and gap identification

In this step of the assessment, you will have an open discussion with your team and come up with your capability rating for the five projects you have selected in Chapter 3, "Business Goals and Initiatives." Please see Chapter 4, "Leadership Assessment," for a detailed example of the process. You will replicate this process for assessing the strengths and weaknesses of your culture toward AI project success.

Figure 8 shows a blank template for you to use. Your five business goals appear down the left side. Across the top are four areas of culture competency. You will fill in the 20 cells with a rating from 1 to 10 with the lowest rating being a 1, which means you are not at all capable with this competency for this initiative, up to a high rating of 10, which means you are fully capable and have no barriers or gaps in this competency to complete the initiative. You will provide the oversight committee with a copy of your completed mapping results.

Example
Business Goals
1 Reduce Manufacturing cost by 5%
2 Cut expense statement processing time to less than 5 days with 95% accuracy
3 Improve Customer Retention by 7%
4 Reduce customer service call times by 10%
5 Improve Customer Satisfaction Score by 6 points

Business Goal	Adaptable and innovative	Continual learning and improvement	Strong team Focus and member maturity	Willingness to risk failure
1				
2				
3				
4				
5				

Figure 8: Scoring Culture–Readiness Mapping Tool Template

Identification of strengths and weakness / potential failure points

The last part of the assessment to pass onto the oversight committee will be a list of strengths and weaknesses that can impact the likelihood of success for the initiative. We outlined a detailed example of this exercise in the last chapter. You should identify key cultural strengths and weaknesses for success with each of the five projects.

Next, we address the contribution of Operations and Structure to AI project success.

References

Bean and Davenport, 2019; Companies are failing in their efforts to become data-driven; https://hbr.org/2019/02/companies-are-failing-in-their-efforts-to-become-data-driven.

Lockwood, T., and Papke, E. (2017). *Innovation by design: How Any Organization Can Leverage Design Thinking to Produce Change, Drive New Ideas, and Deliver Meaningful Solutions.* Red Wheel/Weiser.

Vanderbloemen, W. (2018). *Culture wins: The Roadmap to an Irresistible Workplace.* Savio Republic.

Six

Operations and Structure

"Every Company has two organizational structures; The formal one is written on charts; the other is the everyday relationship of the men and women in the organization"

Harold Geneen

The structure of your organization has an impact on your ability to deliver project results with AI. Flat organizations are typically more nimble, agile, and quicker to adapt than hierarchical ones. Flat organizations are sometimes positively correlated with cultures of open communication and corporate allegiance than hierarchical organizations. Whereas hierarchical organizations tend to be more political.

Operations also affect your ability to run your enterprise with AI methods. We will use operations in a broad sense. If your business is run more by machines, your AI projects will likely be about automation. If humans run your business, then the projects and solutions will look different. We will discuss this more deeply in the next section.

Why operations and structure are important to AI project success

We will briefly discuss why operations matter to AI project success. We will contrast operations suited for automated actions versus more human decision-making operations. When humans make most of the decisions or take most of the actions, we call this human-in-the-loop AI. When operations may be automated, we call this human-out-of-the-loop AI.

AI projects for human-in-the-loop operations

Businesses that have a large human element overseeing internal processes gain significantly from AI which helps those individuals with day-to-day activities. Some examples:

- Automated reports.
- Interactive real-time reports.
- Relevant information at the point of need.
- Visual dashboards.
- Predictive analytics–what is predicted to happen based on inputs.

- Prescriptive analytics–what is recommended you do.
- Corporate language models i.e. AI Chat.

These are all examples where humans have the final decision. However, human intelligence is augmented by some additional intelligence. The key benefit here is faster, better decisions being made.

Some business examples are:

- Facilitate the call center with easily accessible information and smarter routing of calls.
- Handheld devices for warehouse personnel with real-time information.
- Interactive, visual dashboards for sales managers.
- An AI-facilitated report for a radiologist with a likelihood of breast cancer prediction based on mammograms.
- AI recommendations to engineers on what needs to be done on an assembly line to correct an issue of producing products out of specification.
- Large language models like ChatGPT that help marketers with creative content.

AI projects for human-out-of-the-loop operations

Businesses that have operations that are currently labor intensive but could be automated may benefit from AI in that automation process. Many of the same AI techniques mentioned above can be used for the following business examples:

- Automatic sending of an email marketing campaign to the top 5% of customers likely to respond.
- Automate the call center with AI Chat Bots.
- Identify equipment most likely to break down and automatically notify repair specialists.
- Automatic supply fulfillment based on external market information.
- Irrigation control based on sensor and weather data.
- Humanless warehouses. Automated stores and restaurants.

What are your operations like? Can you benefit from human-in-the-loop AI or human-out-of-the-loop AI? Both?

Structure versus culture

There is little debate that corporate success or failure relies heavily upon corporate culture. However, developing an AI culture takes time; changing any culture takes time. One of the immediate things that any organization can do is to optimize its structure to improve the odds of success.

If your organization is very small, it is easy to garner an atmosphere of team / shared values–everyone wins or dies together. If you are part of a biotech startup with ten people, people work together because it is either everyone succeeds and becomes wealthy or everyone fails, and you are out of a job that you have heavily invested yourself in. Your stake is in the outcome of the entire enterprise; the entire enterprise must succeed. Even if you perform very well relative to others, that does not matter because if the ship goes down, everyone goes down with it. Furthermore, your peers must deliver, and therefore, you cheer for them; you do everything you can to make sure they succeed because their success is the collective success, your success. With only ten people, everyone is important!

What happens to an organization of 10,000 people? First, you typically have lots of layers with staff, department managers, directors, senior directors, vice presidents (VPs), senior VPs, and executive VPs. Fancy titles are even created to make people feel more important, because it is easy to get lost in a large organization. Rank matters a great deal.

With rank, politics, posturing, positioning, and games ensue. Life becomes a zero-sum game, meaning I must take someone down for me to win. Backstabbing, turf wars, and petty behavior ensue to make me look better. This is a downside of human nature, but it exists as a defense mechanism—the only way for me to win is for you to lose. This creates real problems in many organizations. What is at stake now is my survival, not the organization's survival, so I will forfeit the good of the organization for what is good for me.

As a leader, you must carefully consider options to mitigate the politics and games in your organization. One thing to consider is providing structure within your organization to promote the good of the whole.

Another example from Texas Instruments was developing the optimal strategy for warehouse and distribution. I was very fortunate to work with extremely talented people on this project. A simplified description of our task was to determine:

1. Should we add distribution centers in North America?

2. If so,

   a. Where were we to locate them?
   b. What size should they be?
   c. What other specifications?

3. Regardless, what are the optimal routes and logistics plans?

We had McKinsey & Company in-house to help with this project. We also had a diverse cross-functional team to help out. Our business unit had a matrix structure. This provided two paths to success for your career: Functional and Program success. Functionally, I was in finance, reporting to the CFO. Program wise, I was head of Decision Support. We supported every executive with analytical problems–design, engineering, manufacturing, customer support, sales, marketing, and finance.

Formulating the project and coming up with a winning solution would have been very difficult without this matrix structure. The project would likely have failed if we had been solely a traditional hierarchical organizational structure. NOTE: That is certainly not true for all AI projects. However, if a project is highly dependent on people from various functions working together as a cohesive team, a matrix or flat organization works best for projects requiring people with diverse skills and knowledge.

Operations and structure assessment for your organization

The following steps are laid out as individual meetings, but you may break these into as many meetings as you see fit. You should plan multiple meetings. The steps appear first. Then a questionnaire and worksheets are provided.

1. Team selection

As mentioned, your team may be uniquely selected for this assessment or contain some of the same members from other assessments. A best practice is to assign a project manager who will be part of each team to provide consistency and continuity.

2. Team education

The goal of this meeting is to educate your team on the AI readiness assessment (ARA) process. Some of the items to discuss are:

- The overall ARA process.
- Information from this chapter
- The five projects to evaluate
- Questions and open discussion
- Goals and agenda for the next meeting

NOTE: Using the original numbering scheme for your AI initiatives/projects is important. These need to be consistent throughout the process. Additionally, you should have summaries of each project, including the functional departments and some of the key members contributing to the project for every initiative.

---

3. Brainstorming and open exchange

This meeting aims to educate your team on the AI readiness assessment (ARA) process. Some of the items to discuss are:

- Review and opening questions and open review discussion
- Operations and organizational structure capabilities questionnaire
- Questions and final thoughts
- Goals and agenda for the next meeting

NOTE: Some organizations meet to discuss the questionnaire, assign it as homework, and then review as a team.

4. Scoring assessment and gap identification

This meeting aims to use the Operations and Organizational Structure Readiness Mapping Tool to rate the organization's ability to execute AI projects. Additionally, to identify potential failure points and gaps for each project. Meeting agenda:

- Open review of last meeting notes and questions
- Complete the operations and organizational structure readiness mapping tool
- Strengths and weakness / potential failure point identification for each project

5. Share findings with oversight committee for aggregation

Instead of a meeting, this is simply turning over the relevant materials to the oversight committee. This committee will be aggregating all functional parts of the ARA.

Questions for discussion

Gather your assessment team and any members of the leadership team and go through the following questions. Record the results.

What are your operations like? Can you benefit from human-in-the-loop AI or human-out-of-the-loop AI? Both?

How has your organization's structure changed with growth?

Would you consider your organization structure siloed? If so, what are the benefits and drawbacks of this structure?

Would you say there is effective communication across different groups and functions within your organization?

Access to people across functions, roles, and hierarchy

How would most staff answer the following? I have ready access to any other employee across roles and functions in the organization.

a) I strongly disagree
b) I disagree
c) I am Neutral
d) I agree Strongly
e) I agree

Would most people say they work with people across multiple departments?

Would most people say they can access people at any level in the organization?

Can people access each other directly for an hour's meeting, or is it protocol to get permission from their manager?

How would most staff answer the following?

Does your function (finance, marketing, IT, accounting, etc.) make it difficult for people to exchange ideas and work together?

Do your hierarchical levels (C Suite, VPs, directors, etc.) make it difficult for people to exchange ideas and work together?

Would most staff agree or disagree with the following statements?

I have been asked questions by a manager in another department.

I am willing to talk with anyone at the company regardless of role or function.

I think we have a very open organization for the exchange of information and ideas.

Repetitive environment or creative environment?

Would you say much of your work is consistent daily, or does it seem that every day brings new challenges?

What tasks are required that can never be automated? Which ones could be automated?

How difficult is it to train new staff? Do you have procedure manuals? How adequate are they for fulfilling most training needs?

Are the daily activities of your workforce creative in nature?

Are the daily activities of your workforce procedural in nature?

Machine-based work or human-based work?

Are most of the work tasks performed in your organization by humans or non-humans (technology or machines)?

Are there decisions made that AI could never effectively make?

Could additional data or the right data improve the quality of decisions in the organization?

Are there decisions that an intelligent agent could make that can be automatically executed?

Do you succeed by automation or increases in human capital?

Do you have a structure that supports human capital or equipment?

Novel environment or conventional environment?

Is the work being done today similar to what was done a year ago? Three Years ago? Five? Or is the work being done constantly changing year by year?

Is your organization creating new job roles and descriptions?

Is your organization getting rid of various job roles?

Would you consider your organization more dynamic, needing to always change? Or would you consider your organization more static, slowly changing over time?

Scoring operations and organizational structure - assessment and gap identification

In this step of the assessment, you will have an open discussion with your team and come up with your capability rating for the five projects you have selected in Chapter 3, "Business Goals and Initiatives."

Please see Chapter 4, "Leadership Assessment," for a detailed example of the process. You will replicate this process for assessing the strengths and weaknesses of your Operations and Organizational Structure toward AI project success.

Figure 9 shows a blank template for you to use. Your five business goals appear down the left side. Across the top are three areas of Operations and Structure competency. You will fill in the 15 cells with a rating from 1 to 10, with the lowest rating being a 1 which means you are not at all capable with this competency for this initiative up to a high rating of 10, which means you are fully capable and have no barriers or gaps in this competency to complete the initiative. You will provide a copy of your completed mapping results to the oversight committee.

Example

Business Goals

1 Reduce Manufacturing cost by 5%
2 Cut expense statement processing time to less than 5 days with 95% accuracy
3 Improve Customer Retention by 7%
4 Reduce customer service call times by 10%
5 Improve Customer Satisfaction Score by 6 points

Business Goal	Functions, Roles and Hierarchy Access	Ability to Adapt/Change for Creativity and Human Capital	Organizational Resiliency
1			
2			
3			
4			
5			

Figure 9: Scoring Operations and Structure–Readiness Mapping Tool Template

Identification of strengths and weakness / potential failure points

The last part of the assessment to send to the oversight committee will be a list of strengths and weaknesses that can impact the likelihood of success for the initiative. We outlined a detailed example of this exercise in Chapter 4. You should identify your key strengths and weaknesses for success with each of the five projects.

Next, we address the contribution of Industry and Market to AI project success.

SEVEN

Industry and Market Assessment

> *"A corporation is a living organism; it has to continue to shed its skin. Methods have to change. Focus has to change. Values have to change. The sum total of those changes is transformation."*
>
> *Andrew Grove*

The industry in which you compete correlates with the problems you face and your approach to solving them. At a high level, there are slowly changing industries with very consistent processes and market forces. Then, there are newer, highly evolving industries that require dynamic approaches. Some industries require a lot of human intervention and decision making, and others do not.

Your industry and market will have a major impact on the AI projects you wish to pursue. We discussed this in Chapter 3, "Business Goals and Initiatives." Some industries use AI for the majority of their activities. Other industries

125

might use AI deeply, but only in narrow parts of the firm. Still, others are just beginning to take a step forward in AI.

AI pushes the GDP higher, but there are differences across industries. According to Microsoft, a study by PWC calculated that global GDP will be 14 percent higher by 2030 as a result of AI adoption, which will contribute an additional $15.7 trillion to the global economy.

To dig deeper into the business impact AI can bring to specific industries like manufacturing, retail, health care, financial services, and the public sector, Microsoft commissioned The Economist Intelligence Unit report, "Intelligent economies: AI's transformation of industries and societies," which surveyed more than 400 senior executives working in various industries across eight markets. The study aims to help educate business leaders on the significant potential of AI across industries and countries. Respondents are optimistic about the economic benefits that AI will bring. Over the next five years, survey respondents expect AI to have a positive impact on growth (90%), productivity (86%), innovation (84%), and job creation (69%). (The Economist, Intelligent Economies: AI's transformation of industries and society)

Why industry and market are important to AI project success

AI is not going away. It will likely be overhyped and misunderstood, but it has a huge impact on how businesses operate. That impact will accelerate in the coming years.

If your competition is not actively using AI, they will soon. The adoption of AI and technology is highly influenced by industry and market forces. As we said, this could be a local part of the business or across the business. It could be with simpler or more advanced forms of AI, but your competition will be using AI soon. If you want to stay competitive, you will have to do the same.

Your industry and market will affect which AI projects you decide to take on. One advantage of AI-driven decision making is the ability to create winning plans and strategies.

Industry affects regulation, compliance, and more

AI has the ability to impact different industries in different ways. Consider the differences between low regulation industries versus highly regulated ones. Highly regulated industries are controlled by hundreds of regulatory bodies. Keeping up with all the policy and rule changes and keeping compliant is a daunting task. Heavily regulated bodies are now looking toward AI for help. For example, consider what Forbes said about **Environment, Health, and Safety (EHS)**:

"**Safe Working Environments With AI.** In 2018, more than 5,000 workers in the U.S. died at their workplace. In the same year, the expenses on occupational injuries and accidental deaths in the U.S. amounted to almost $171 billion, according to the National Safety Council. To protect employees' health and well-being, companies have to transform workspaces and take care of their employees. When combined with other related technologies, AI is able to augment the human workforce, allowing EHS professionals to proactively manage various EHS risks and create a safe workplace environment for employees."

Industry and market affect AI projects

Your organization makes small decisions and large decisions. You should take extra time and care on these large decisions and AI can help. One of the biggest risks a firm can undertake is strategic planning. Where should we invest? What is the risk? What is the reward? There are huge dollars on the table. There are multiple objectives and multiple concerns.

As I mentioned previously, we faced a large, expensive question when I was at Texas Instruments (TI). Should we alter our business unit's logistics and distribution strategy? I was very fortunate to work with extremely talented people on this project. A simplified description of our task was to determine:

1. Should we add distribution centers in North America?

2. If so,
   a. Where should we locate them?
   b. What size should they be?
   c. What other specifications should we consider?
   d. What would they cost?

3. Regardless, we must optimize our routes. What is the plan?

If we made poor decisions, it would likely have one or more of the following impacts:

1. We would waste $ millions on construction.

2. We would have ineffective logistics, costing $ millions per year.

3. Our competition would be delivering products cheaper so that we would have a cost disadvantage. They could potentially undercut us.

4. It could delay our deliveries and speed was everything in delivering products in a highly competitive market.

Two reasons this was an important project. *Our Industry and our market.* Our industry was consumer products: calculators, notebook computers, and laser printers. Distribution was an enormous cost for the business, so we needed to do the best we could. *We needed to be quick, and we needed to be cheap.*

We had a smart, diverse, and cross-functional team to work on this project, and I led the effort. This was a tremendous responsibility with huge risks. The first part of this project was a one-time shot. Would we build or not. We could not undo this decision.

The second part of the project was routing, which could be altered over time. However, if we got the first decision wrong, we would never achieve an optimal routing solution.

Our AI solution was paired with two methodologies. On the front end, we developed simulation models based on our internal data, market data, and our estimates. A single scenario would pass the inputs into a mathematical (linear) programming method that produced routes and cost estimates. We would store results and then create another scenario and repeat the process. We did this over and over until we had an entire solution space to make our decision.

We built a new distribution center on the West Coast. We formulated a very slick system to optimize the routing schedule. From all the information we could gather, we had the most efficient and lowest-cost distribution network in North America. Another proof point was that after we exited the notebook business, Dell was very eager to snap up our logistics team, and our team leader became the worldwide leader of Dell's Supply and Logistics division.

Industry and market assessment for your organization

The following steps are laid out as individual meetings, but you may break these into as many meetings as you see fit. You should plan multiple meetings. The steps are laid out first. Then, a questionnaire and worksheets are provided.

1. Team selection

As mentioned, your team may be uniquely selected for this assessment or contain some of the same members from other assessments. A best practice is to assign a project manager who will be part of each team to provide consistency and continuity.

2. Team education

The goal of this meeting is to educate your team on the AI readiness assessment (ARA) process. Items to discuss are:

- The overall ARA process
- Information from this chapter
- The five projects being evaluated
- Questions and open discussion
- Goals and agenda for the next meeting

NOTE: Using the original numbering scheme for your AI initiatives/projects is important. These need to be consistent throughout the process. Additionally, you should have summaries of each project, including the functional departments and some of the key members contributing to the project for every initiative.

3. Brainstorming and open exchange

The goal of this meeting is to educate your team on the AI readiness assessment (ARA) process. Some of the items to discuss are:

- Review and opening questions and open review discussion
- Industry and market structure capabilities questionnaire
- Questions and final thoughts
- Goals and agenda for the next meeting

NOTE: Some organizations meet to discuss the questionnaire and then assign it as homework to be reviewed as a team.

An assessment tool is offered in the following section, "Industry and Market Questionnaire–Step 3."

---

4. Scoring assessment and gap identification

This meeting aims to use the Operations and Organizational Structure Readiness mapping tool to rate leaders' ability to execute AI projects. Additionally, to identify potential failure points and gaps for each project. Meeting agenda:

- Open review of last meeting notes and questions
- Complete the industry and market readiness mapping tool
- Strengths and weakness / potential failure point identification for each project

You will find an example of a Readiness Mapping Tool template in the following section, "Industry and Market Scoring."

5. Share findings with oversight committee for aggregation

Instead of a meeting, this is simply turning over the relevant materials to the oversight committee. This committee will be aggregating all functional parts of the ARA.

Questions for discussion

Gather your assessment team and any members of the leadership team and go through the following questions. Record the results.

How stable is your industry? Rapidly evolving or near static in nature?

Is your market highly competitive? What are the drivers of competition? Innovation? Price? Customer service? Product or service quality?

Do you have new competition coming into your territory? This could be out of the area, state, or country entering your territory. If so, has this been accelerating? Do you have plans to address it?

Are parts of your industry being replaced by new technology or new business models? How are you addressing this issue? Vying to compete? Exiting those areas?

Industry standards and processes

Do you have to comply with certain industry standards that are rigid and set (mandated)?

Are there general norms everyone in your industry follows or adheres to (not mandated)?

Do you have routine audits by external organizations? Do you bear a significant cost complying with and performing these audits?

Industry and market education and innovation

Do your leaders, managers, or staff read industry trade journals to keep up to date with developments?

What sources of information are you using to determine how your market is changing? What are you doing to address those changes? Are you adapting quickly enough?

Name a project that you have completed recently that has been taken on as a response to industry trends or market forces.

Ability to respond to outside forces

Have you had a reorganization or reduction in force in response to a change in your *market*? What was the change in the market? How long did it take to identify? How did you identify it? Who identified it? How long did it take to decide after recognizing something happening that needed to be addressed? How long did it take to implement the change? How was the news received? How long did it take for the organization to get back to normal?

Have you had a reorganization or reduction in force in response to a shift in your *industry*? What was the trend? How long did it take to identify? How did you identify it? Who identified it? How long did it take to decide after recognizing something happening that needed to be addressed? How long did it take to implement the change? How was the news received? How long did it take for the organization to get back to normal?

Scoring industry and market - assessment and gap identification

In this step of the assessment, you will have an open discussion with your team and come up with your capability rating for the five projects you have selected in Chapter 3, "Business Goals and Initiatives."

Please see Chapter 4, "Leadership Assessment," for a detailed example of the process. You will replicate this process for assessing the strengths and weaknesses of your Industry and Market toward AI project success.

Figure 10 shows a blank template for you to use. Your five business goals appear down the left side. Across the top are two areas of Industry and Market competency. You will fill in the 10 cells with a rating from 1 to 10 , with the lowest rating being a 1, which means you are not at all capable with this competency for this initiative up to a high rating of 10, which means you are fully capable and have no barriers or gaps in this competency to complete the initiative. You will provide a copy of your completed mapping results to the oversight committee.

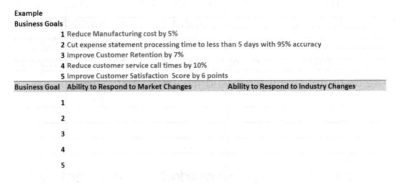

Example
Business Goals

1	Reduce Manufacturing cost by 5%
2	Cut expense statement processing time to less than 5 days with 95% accuracy
3	Improve Customer Retention by 7%
4	Reduce customer service call times by 10%
5	Improve Customer Satisfaction Score by 6 points

Business Goal	Ability to Respond to Market Changes	Ability to Respond to Industry Changes
1		
2		
3		
4		
5		

Figure 10: Scoring Industry and Market - Readiness Mapping Tool Template

Identification of strengths and weakness / potential failure points

The last part of the assessment to send to the oversight committee will be a list of strengths and weaknesses that can impact the likelihood of success for the initiative. We outlined a detailed example of this exercise in Chapter 4. You should identify your key strengths and weaknesses for success with each of the five projects.

Next, we address the contribution of People to AI project success.

EIGHT

People Assessment

"The future belongs to those who learn more skills and combine them in creative ways."

Robert Greene

This chapter is about people. We want to discuss your entire ecosystem of people and professionals that add value to your organization. Your direct employees, meaning people on your payroll. And indirect employees may include consultants, temporary workers, contract workers, or anyone you can bring in to get the job done.

This part of the assessment will focus on skills, abilities, knowledge, and aptitude. We distinguish this from culture. There, we say, "Organizational culture is the shared values, customs, traditions, rituals, behaviors, and beliefs shared by the members of that organization." We will also distinguish it from how the organization organizes its people in Chapter 6, "Operations and Structure."

It is very important to understand your existing team's ability to successfully complete your AI projects. This allows you to:

- Judicially decide on which projects to undertake.
- Fill existing gaps from the outside in the short term.
- Educate your existing staff for the longer term.
- Supplement your team with strategic hiring for the longer term.

Why people are important to AI project success

You are familiar with the cliché. "People are our most important asset." It is true. As people make the important decisions, AI can make decisions, too, but as of this writing, they are second-tier decisions. Figure 11 illustrates our previous notion that people are the center of the six foundations of AI success.

The reason that 'People' is in the center of Figure 11 is that people influence everything. Who you hire, train, nurture, and promote influences everything. Your people are your organization.

We want to focus on core strengths that lead to success. If you lack them, it will be harder to succeed. In the end, the evaluation of what you have and what you need is a critical exercise. Once you have completed the exercise, you can remedy the situation in various ways, as mentioned above.

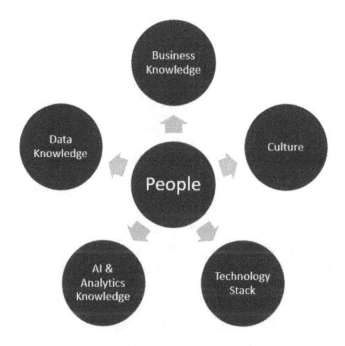

Figure 11: The Six Foundations of the Success of AI Programs

Here are the critical skills we want to focus on for this portion of the assessment.

- Skills
- Knowledge
- Aptitude / Ability to Learn
- Willingness to Learn
- An open mind
- Emotional Intelligence
- Desire to make positive changes.
- Drive, tenacity, and willingness to succeed.
- Attitude! Team Wins, We Win, I Win Attitude

As you move through a new paradigm, having strong LOCAL leaders (i.e., champions) is important.

These are *pioneers* you need to help others through the process. These pioneers are early adopters with knowledge, skills, and good leadership abilities.

The importance of domain knowledge

Domain knowledge is understanding an area of activity or a subject. We are concerned with business knowledge. That knowledge is unique to your organization. What should people know about your business to make the best decision? What actions do they take, and what understanding do they need to take the best action.

The business knowledge of your people is at least as important, if not more important, than data and AI acumen. If you cannot translate a problem into measurable business terms, you will have limited success in solving it. To do this, you need both sets of skills. Your people may be stronger on one side or the other, but you should have some people who have both. Otherwise, it is difficult to translate the core business problem into a quantifiable AI project, see Figure 12.

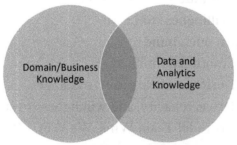

Figure 12: People with Business Knowledge, Analytics Knowledge, and a Combination of both.

CoPs strengthen data and AI literacy

Creating a community of practice (CoP) is a great way to promote data literacy and AI adoption. This can be a functional CoP–marketing, finance, operations, etc. where you have informal meetings and share the best ideas. This should be encouraged, but voluntary. It will identify true believers in analytics and AI.

This can also be an organizational analytics and AI CoP where interested parties across functions attend meetings and share/demonstrate what they are doing in their departments. This promotes idea sharing and cross-group education. It also provides for interdepartmental career movement.

True benefits of diversity

When I was at Zilliant, a B2B pricing optimization company, I worked on the pricing science team. This team was essentially a group of people that were good at math, computers, problem solving, and the like. My boss had compiled the smartest, most diverse team I ever worked on. This diversity was defined by:

- Education
- Professional Experience
- Global Geography

This diversity contributed to the success of the team.

There were 14 members of the team, and each had formal education and advanced degrees across many disciplines, including statistics, operations research, industrial engineering, computer science, economics, physics, mathematics, business, and natural sciences. Each of us had an aptitude to learn and a willingness to learn. Each member believed skills and knowledge were important to their career and personally invested heavily in them. Each educational discipline had a unique way of looking at a problem and the collaboration was rich and fulfilling.

We had different professional experiences which contributed to our success. For example, it contributed to defining the problems we faced and all the necessary parameters and then searching across our experience set to formulate potential solutions.

Everyone had an open mind. If someone could convince you they had a better idea, it would be a good exchange, and people would come around. This is a sign of emotional intelligence. We were okay with killing our darlings and coming around to a new way of thinking. Why? Because we knew that if the team won, the individuals would win. We had a desire to come up with great solutions. We had a team drive to succeed. We had winning skills, a winning attitude, and a winning team.

People assessment for your organization

The following steps are laid out as individual meetings, but you may break these into as many meetings as you see fit.

You should plan multiple meetings. The steps are laid out first. Then a questionnaire and worksheets are provided.

---

1. Team selection

As mentioned previously, your team may be uniquely selected for this assessment or contain some of the same members from other assessments. A best practice is to assign a project manager who will be part of each team to provide consistency and continuity.

---

2. Team education

This meeting aims to educate your team on the AI readiness assessment (ARA) process. Some of the items to discuss:

- The overall ARA process
- Information from this chapter
- The five projects being evaluated
- Questions and open discussion
- Goals and agenda for the next meeting

NOTE: Using the original numbering scheme for your AI initiatives/projects is important. These need to be consistent throughout the process. Additionally, you should have summaries of each project, including the functional departments and some of the key members contributing to the project for every initiative.

---

3. Brainstorming and open exchange

This meeting aims to educate your team on the AI readiness assessment (ARA) process. Some of the items to discuss

- Review and opening questions and open review discus
- People capabilities questionnaire
- Questions and final thou
- Goals and agenda for the next meeting

NOTE: Some organizations meet to discuss the questionnaire and then assign it as homework to be reviewed as a team. An assessment tool is offered in the following section, "People Assessment Questionnaire–Step 3."

---

4. Scoring assessment and gap identification

This meeting aims to use the People Readiness mapping tool to rate the organizations' ability to execute AI projects. Additionally, to identify potential failure points and gaps for each project. Meeting age

- Open review of last meeting notes and quest
- Complete the people readiness assessment mapping
- Strengths and weakness / potential failure point identification for each project

You will find an example of a Readiness Mapping Tool template in the following section, " People Assessment Scoring."

5. Share findings with oversight committee for aggregation

Instead of a meeting, this is simply turning over the relevant materials to the oversight committee. This committee will be aggregating all ARA functional parts.

Questions for discussion

Gather your assessment team and any members of the leadership team and go through the following questions. Record the results.

If you were to ask the 'average' employee, would they say they have 'great faith' or 'little faith' in their fellow employee's ability to get today's job done? If you were to ask the 'average' employee, would they say they have 'great faith' or 'little faith' in their fellow employee's ability to make the place better for tomorrow? Name examples of people lacking skills, abilities, or attitudes to succeed. What were the deficiencies? If you could fill the gaps, what would have made the difference?

Skills and knowledge

How would you compare your employee's skills to your competition?

Has your business suffered a real loss or a loss of opportunity by people lacking the skills to successfully correct for it? What was the lack?

Do you have anything like a CoP mentioned in this chapter? Or lunch and learns or anything similar?

How would you rate your people's business communication skills?

How would you rate your people's business literacy skills?

How would you rate your people's data knowledge? Their data IT skills?

How would you rate your people's analytics and AI knowledge? Their IT skills?

How would you rate your people's familiarity and competency in general usage of company technology?

Is there a strong IT department? What are their best skills?

How would you rate your people's general business acumen?

Do your employees have the ability to formulate business problems into data-solvable problems?

Do your people have an overall understanding of the business or just their limited areas?

How would you rate your people's problem design skills? How well can they translate a business problem into a technical construction?

Has your business been harmed by unforeseen events that were due to a lack of knowledge or aptitude? What were the events? What were the gaps?

Do employees have sufficient knowledge to work independently or rely on others for constant help?

Aptitude / willingness to learn

Has your business suffered a loss due to your people lacking the ability to successfully learn what they should have known to address the challenge?

Would your people say they are given all the right tools and support to do their job well?

What abilities do your employees need to learn? Are they capable of learning them?

How would you rate your people's ability to adapt to new situations?

How would you rate your people's ability to learn?

How would you rate your people's ability to contribute?

Would you say the people in your organization are eager to keep learning, or once they can maintain their job level, they would rather stay 'status quo'?

Do you have to push people into training or are they asking for training?

Do you offer internal training for employees?

Do you offer educational assistance or tuition reimbursement for employees in education programs outside of the office?

Do you have any other training or growth programs for employees to improve their skill sets?

Open mindedness

Would you say people are open to new ideas? Are they open to new ways of approaching things?

Would you say people tend to stick to their opinions? Or are they open to a discussion and rational evaluation of other people's opinions?

Have you had a bad business outcome that could have been avoided if people were just willing to listen?

Emotional intelligence

Has your business suffered a real loss or a loss of opportunity by people attacking each other rather than tackling the problem? What were the issues?

Do you need to constantly manage people's feelings?

Would you say people are more interested in what *other* people are doing or what *they* are doing?

Are people supportive of each other?

How would you rate your people's ability to adapt and learn new processes?

How would you rate your people's willingness to change?

Desire to make positive changes

Are your people independent and resourceful? Can they get special project work done without much supervision or do they need constant attention? Do you have to ride them to get the work done?

Do your people want to make changes that have a positive impact on the organization, or do they just want to do their job and get home as soon as possible?

Do employees that have moved on and left the company for whatever reason ever come back to your offices for a visit?

Drive, tenacity, and willingness to succeed

Do your employees have a workspace that is conducive to their work? Are employees happy in their workspace? Is it conducive to them wanting to come to work?

What will you find your people doing when no one is watching?

How motivated are your people to win new business? Do they work hard to deliver great results for customers?

Would you say your employees have a competitive spirit? Do they desire to beat the competition?

Team attitude

Would you say people are more interested in advancing themselves over others or advancing the organization knowing they are a part of that organization?

How would you rate your people's desire to be a team player?

How would you rate your people's knowledge of the interdependency and interplay of the business functions?

How would you rate your people's overall attitude?

Scoring people - assessment and gap identification

In this step of the assessment, you will have an open discussion with your team and come up with your capability rating for the five projects you have selected in Chapter 3, "Business Goals and Initiatives."

Please see Chapter 4, "Leadership Assessment," for a detailed example of the process. You will replicate this process for assessing the strengths and weaknesses of your People toward AI project success.

Figure 13 shows a blank template for you to use. Your five business goals appear down the left side. Across the top are four areas of People competency. You will fill in the 20 cells with a rating from 1 to 10 , with the lowest rating being a 1 which means you are not at all capable with this competency for this initiative up to a high rating of 10, which means you are fully capable and have no barriers or gaps in this competency to complete the initiative. You will provide a copy of your completed mapping results to the oversight committee.

Example
Business Goals
1 Reduce Manufacturing cost by 5%
2 Cut expense statement processing time to less than 5 days with 95% accuracy
3 Improve Customer Retention by 7%
4 Reduce customer service call times by 10%
5 Improve Customer Satisfaction Score by 6 points

Business Goal	Skills and Knowledge	Aptitude / Willingness to Learn	Open Mindedness and Emotional Intelligence	Drive and Attitude to Succeed
1				
2				
3				
4				
5				

Figure 13: Scoring People–Readiness Mapping Tool Template

Identification of strengths and weakness / potential failure points

The last part of the assessment to send to the oversight committee will be a list of strengths and weaknesses that can impact the likelihood of success for the initiative. We outlined a detailed example of this exercise in Chapter 4. You should identify your key strengths and weaknesses for success with each of the five projects.

Next, we address the contribution of Data to AI project success.

NINE

Data Assessment

> "It is a capital mistake to theorize before one has data."
>
> Sherlock Holmes in A study in Scarlet

Data is the life blood of modern business. Data is everywhere. Data is in your mind, in your experience, in your corporate systems. And data relevant to you even exists outside of your organization. You cannot make informed decisions without data. The data assessment is based upon several factors, including:

1) the organization's current data *capture* and storage
2) the *consistency* and *quality* of that data
3) the *availability* of that data to stakeholders
4) the *security*, *governance*, and *compliance* with regulatory agencies
5) the *sustainability* of data streams

The data assessments are performed with an evaluation tool completed by leaders, managers, and identified stakeholders, especially IT and their representatives. The assessment tool rates the ability of the current data architecture and associated technology to execute the top five business initiatives and determine gaps and weaknesses.

Companies experience the most challenges when leveraging AI alongside their data. In fact, 81% of respondents admit that this is due to data existing in silos across their organizations, according to a 2023 TDWI survey.

While data serves as the backbone for AI operations, it is also the area where readiness is the weakest, with the greatest number of Laggards (17%) compared to other pillars. 81% of all respondents claim some degree of siloed or fragmented data in their organization.

This poses a critical challenge. The complexity of integrating data in various sources affects the use and advantage of AI.

NOTE: One of the major weaknesses of data readiness is the lack of data literacy or data knowledge. This part of the assessment is found in the last chapter, Chapter 8, "People Assessment" as it is part of knowledge, skills, and aptitude.

Why data is important to AI project success

Data reflects a process or series of actions or steps taken to achieve a particular end goal. Life is all about processes. We have biological and chemical processes that govern our health and well-being. We have business processes that impact the success or failure of our business. Anything that you desire to understand or improve involves a process. **Data is just the artifacts of a process.** Therefore, data are key to any consciously based improvement.

Data is the Cornerstone of Improvement. You cannot improve what you do not measure.

You cannot even determine how you are doing until you compare at least two data points. "Everything is relative" is attributed to Albert Einstein. All assessments are based on comparisons, relating two or more things. We make thousands of comparisons daily to determine our relative progress toward our stated or unstated goals and intentions. That is why data is so important.

Data is at the heart of

- Maintaining status quo
- Improving on the status quo
- Answering, "How am I doing?"

Data challenges are often due to one or more of the "Data V's."

A classification that makes it easier to understand the challenges with data can be described by the five V's of data:

- **Data volume.** Data volume is the sheer amount of data. The volume is daunting and overwhelming, and most of it goes unused. It should be of great value. Yet, collecting data is just a cost if you are not using it.

- **Data variety.** Data variety describes the diverse data sources, data types, structures, and formats of data.

- **Data velocity.** Data velocity describes how fast data is being added to systems and how often it is refreshed.

- **Data value.** Data value is the return on investment (ROI) for sourcing, transforming, securing, and protecting data. Collecting, storing, and securing data is a huge cost. Therefore, the only way to get a positive return on data is to offset this cost by applying and operationalizing AI.

- **Data veracity.** Data veracity is the quality, reliability, and trustworthiness of the data. Data quality is one of the biggest limiting factors in business today.

Data for AI projects

We will not dive deep into all the various forms of data and related technologies, but we will discuss some basics. Why? People have limited views when they think of data. Some think it is technology. Some think it is only what is stored in a data warehouse or the cloud. In reality, data is all around us, including our brains.

Types of data

There are many types of data. We do not store all this data. We forget that data is everywhere—even in our minds. Data is simply a reflection of events. The most valuable use of data in our organizations is the data from our processes. We can use this data to better understand our processes and improve them to better our business. What types of data exist in your business? Think broadly, including text, which is often very useful for AI projects like customer sentiment. Examples:

- Emails, IMs, and electronic conversations
- Social Media
- Corporate contracts
- Call center recordings—written and voice
- Medical records
- Warranty claims, Insurance Claims
- Notes and free text in multiple systems

Locations of data

Data in local systems and applications—servers, PCs, notebooks, phones. Examples are applications that run your business—financial and accounting systems, spreadsheets, CRM systems, ERP systems, and engineering.

Access to useful data

For data to be useful, it must be accessible and useful. How difficult is it for you to get your data? Who has access and how do different people get it? Once they access it, is it useable? This means is it reasonably clean and accurate?

Customer service

At Overstock, we were a pure-play internet retailer, meaning we had no physical storefront locations (no bricks, just clicks). Without seeing and talking with customers, the only understanding we had from our customers was what was captured via our customer touchpoints–the systems where we communicated in one way or another with our customers. It was critical to use this data to understand our customers.

We had to be very responsive to customers and their needs, or we would lose those customers to Amazon or brick-and-mortar stores. Estimates differ, but it is generally accepted that the cost of acquiring an online customer is 1.5 to 2.5 times greater than the initial sale. It is, therefore, essential to keep customers satisfied and retain them so that they become profitable customers for the enterprise.

One of our critical customer touchpoints was the option to call in or email customer service. We had a system where customers could send emails with information, and our customer service agents would respond if necessary. However, it would have done more harm than good if we had made it easy for customers to contact us, yet we were slow to respond, especially with angry customers. Therefore, we created an AI-enabled system to help these customer service agents. Specifically, we created an automated scoring system that evaluated the emotional content of customers based on emails, call center notes, and other data.

By measuring customer sentiment based on data from our customer contact points plus cross-referencing additional internal data sources, we could deploy personnel to address the most important issues. We also improved efficiency by linking internal knowledge sources to email so that the agent could quickly respond with relevant information. Then, we had workflow and operation reports to help us continually improve.

Data assessment for your organization

The following steps are laid out as individual meetings, but you may break these into as many meetings as you see fit. You should plan multiple meetings. The steps are laid out first. Then a questionnaire and worksheets are provided.

---

1. Team selection

As mentioned previously, your team may be uniquely selected for this assessment or contain some of the same members from other assessments. A best practice is to assign a project manager that will be part of each team to provide consistency and continuity.

2. Team education

This meeting aims to educate your team on the AI readiness assessment (ARA) process. Some of the items to discuss

- The overall ARA process
- Information from this chapter
- The five projects being evaluated
- Questions and open discussion
- Goals and agenda for the next meeting

NOTE: Using the original numbering scheme for your AI initiatives/projects is important. These need to be consistent throughout the process. Additionally, you should have summaries of each project, including the functional departments and some of the key members contributing to the project for every initiative.

3. Brainstorming and open exchange

This meeting aims to educate your team on the AI readiness assessment (ARA) process. Some of the items to discuss

- Review and Opening Questions and Open Review Discussion
- Data Capabilities Questionnaire
- Questions and Final Thoughts
- Goals and Agenda for the Next Meeting

NOTE: Some organizations meet to discuss the questionnaire and then assign it as homework to be reviewed as a team.

An assessment tool is offered in the following section, "Data Assessment Questionnaire–Step 3."

---

4. Scoring assessment and gap identification

This meeting aims to use the Data Readiness mapping tool to rate the organizations' ability to execute AI projects. Additionally, to identify potential failure points and gaps for each project. Meeting agenda:

- Open Review of Last Meeting Notes and Questions
- Complete the Data Readiness Assessment Mapping Tool
- Strengths and Weakness / Potential Failure Point Identification for each Project

You will find an example of a Readiness Mapping Tool template in the following section, "Data Assessment Scoring."

---

5. Share findings with oversight committee for aggregation

Instead of a meeting, this is simply turning over the relevant materials to the oversight committee. This committee will be aggregating all functional parts of the ARA.

Questions for discussion

Gather your assessment team and any members of the leadership team and go through the following questions. Record the results.

Data as a strategic asset

Is your organization data driven? Do you make decisions based on data? Do people come into meetings and support their position with data they have gathered or accessed?

On a scale 1 to 10, is your organization data driven? (1 = we never use data to take action or make decisions, 10 = we always use data to take action or make decisions)

Do you have leaders or managers actively trying to get the organization to use data more in decision making? Would you say you have data champions?

How do you compare to your competition in the use of data and related technology?

What are the biggest holdbacks for you to make more use of data related technology?

Investment made in data technology

Does your organization have a technology budget set aside for the acquisition and storage of data? Or is it lumped into a broader budget?

Would you say your data related technology expenditures are rising, falling, or staying flat over time?

Do you feel it is a sufficient investment?

Are you investing in newer technology like cloud technology or services?

Are you using APIs or microservices to capture data?

Is your data volume rising, falling, or staying flat over time?

What percent of your data-related personnel are hired versus contracted?

Investment made on human support of data

Do you have designated people whose sole job is to acquire, store, or use data? For example, data architects, data modelers, database administrators, and data analysts.

Do you hire consultants or contract employees to work on data-related technology and initiatives?

Would you say your data-related employee or consultant expenditures are rising, falling, or staying flat over time?

Do you feel it is a sufficient investment? Are you planning on hiring or contracting more help in the next few years? What about your competition, are they spending more?

Do you have a dedicated data engineer?

Is IT responsible for data or is data part of people's job descriptions?

Data quality and consistency

Do you have a data governance group or program? If so, is this group responsible for data quality? Do you have data stewards or people who are responsible for certain data sources (ERP, HR, Operations, etc.)?

For the data sets that matter, do you have data set owners? Do they ensure the quality and accessibility of this data to the right people? Are these owners outside of IT (i.e., in the business)?

Do you have an individual responsible for data quality?

What is your confidence in the quality of your data? Is the quality sufficient to support all your current day-to-day operational needs? Is it sufficient to support strategic planning? If you have them, is it sufficient to support your business intelligence and AI projects?

Data availability to personnel

Do you have a centralized repository for data where people across the organization can access it? Do you have a data warehouse? Do you have a data lake? Do you have a data lakehouse?

Do you have a data catalog where people can access corporate data? A data collaboration platform. A data virtualization platform?

Do you have a data intelligence platform where people can access corporate data? A data integration platform?

A cloud-based data platform where people can access their data like data-as-a-service?

Data security, governance, and compliance

Do you have procedures or protocols in place for data security? Is it part of your data governance program?

Does your industry or market have strict compliance or regulatory standards? How well is your organization doing? What are any gaps?

Scoring data - assessment and gap identification

This is Step 4, (summarized in the previous overview section). In this step of the assessment, you will have an open discussion with your team and come up with your capability rating for the five projects you have selected in Chapter 3, "Business Goals and Initiatives."

Please see Chapter 4, "Leadership Assessment" for a detailed example of the process. You will replicate this process for assessing the strengths and weaknesses of your corporate data toward AI project success.

Figure 14 shows a blank template for you to use. Your five business goals appear down the left side. Across the top are four areas of data competency. You will fill in the 20 cells with a rating from 1 to 10 , with the lowest rating being a 1 which means you are not at all capable with this competency for this initiative up to a high rating of 10, which means you are fully capable and have no barriers or gaps in this competency to complete the initiative. You will provide a copy of your completed mapping results to the oversight committee.

Example
Business Goals

    1 Reduce Manufacturing cost by 5%
    2 Cut expense statement processing time to less than 5 days with 95% accuracy
    3 Improve Customer Retention by 7%
    4 Reduce customer service call times by 10%
    5 Improve Customer Satisfaction Score by 6 points

Business Goal	Data as a Strategic Asset	Investment Made in Data	Data Quality and Consistency	Data Availability
1				
2				
3				
4				
5				

Figure 14: Scoring Data Competency - Readiness Mapping Tool Template

Identification of strengths and weakness / potential failure points

The last part of the assessment to send to the oversight committee will be a list of strengths and weaknesses that can impact the likelihood of success for the initiative. We outlined a detailed example of this exercise in Chapter 4.

You should identify your key strengths and weaknesses for success with each of the five projects.

Next, we address the contribution of Data to AI project success.

References

Burk, S., and Miner, G. D. (2020). *It's All Analytics! : the foundations of AI, big data, and data science landscape for professionals in healthcare, business, and government.* CRC Press.

TEN

AI Technology Assessment

"The real power of data lies not in its abundance but in our ability to extract meaning from it through AI."

Unknown

This chapter covers the final assessment of your organization's AI readiness. We then provide some examples and things to consider, and we move forward with the assessment assignment just as we have in the last six chapters.

AI technology refers to the data transformation, translation, and modeling of data. This could be any technology that enables enhanced human-assisted decision making (human-in-the-loop decisioning), such as visual displays of data, business intelligence (BI), and third-party applications with embedded suggestions, graphics, or reports. It could be self-service reporting, BI, or AI. It may be complex or as simple as spreadsheets.

The second type of AI technology is automated decision-making or human out-of-the-loop decision making. This is where actions are taken in response to machine learning or other AI models automatically either sending an action to be taken by another machine or representative.

The AI technology assessments are performed with an evaluation tool completed by leaders, managers, and identified stakeholders, especially IT and their representatives. The assessment tool rates the ability of the current AI architecture and associated technology to execute the top five business initiatives and determine gaps and weaknesses.

Some specific examples of AI technology are any software system, platform, or method for

- Advanced Business Reporting and Data Querying
- Business Intelligence (BI) Reporting
- Visual BI, dashboarding, visualization including geo-analytics, mapping (data to images or video)
- Machine Learning, Deep Learning
- Descriptive, Predictive, and Prescriptive analytics
- Statistical Analysis, Engineering Analysis, Simulation

The bottom line is any technology that uses data to improve understanding or action taking.

NOTE: Again, keep in mind, we are not addressing one of the major weaknesses in being AI ready. That is, the lack of

AI literacy or data knowledge in this chapter. This part of the assessment is found in Chapter 8, "People Assessment" as it is part of knowledge, skills, and aptitude.

Why an AI technology assessment is important to AI project success

We have spoken about the power of data and analytics literacy. Knowledge and skills. However, you can greatly leverage that knowledge, even finite knowledge, with the right tools. Not everyone has to be a master of AI to make use of AI. Over the last several years, a major push in the AI space is data and AI democratization. Data-as-a-service was mentioned in the last chapter to provide all stakeholders with easy access to valuable data. We now introduce AI-as-a-service to provide all stakeholders with easy access to AI technology that makes them more efficient and effective in creating forms of AI.

AI-as-a-service technology ensures that everyone that needs AI tools has easy access to them. And the platform is role enabled with the right tools for their particular job. If a company has a "self-service" approach to analytics and AI, it can accelerate adoption and add value for the company.

The importance of partner relationships

Depending on where you are in your analytic maturity there will come a time when you are engaged in two activities that require you to get outside help.

The first is vendor selection of an AI or analytics technology platform or tool set. The second is when you acquire a solution integrator or consulting company to scale more quickly or provide knowledge you lack internally. The type of arrangement you have with these providers greatly affects the probability of project success.

In speaking with a colleague that had years of experience providing AI strategy and solutions, an important success factor came to light. I asked him, "In your opinion, what makes for a successful AI engagement?" He responded, "It is very clear. When we are brought in as partners, these engagements are very successful. When we are brought in as a third party, it is not successful." When the client wanted a partner that provided an environment of trust, mutual effort, and success, the project was successful. When the client saw the vendor or consultant as someone just wanting to make money, it failed.

Make sure you select vendors and consultants that want to be a partner, not a provider. Make sure they want long-term success and a relationship, not a transactional arrangement.

Buying a packaged analytics or mobile app solution *is* an AI project

To be clear, your analytics project solutions do not have to be home grown. Or built internally. There are great prepackaged analytics software platforms and mobile apps available. This is a common entry point into AI. A purchase of a complete prepackaged solution. You may be using them already.

However, *you should treat any prepackaged solution as any other AI project.* It should be treated as one component of a larger project. You should start with a need and then search for the solution. Some vendors will attempt to sell you a solution and tell you that you have a problem.

If you want to purchase an analytics solution, you should run it through an entire AI readiness assessment. Just because it is a canned solution does not mean it will be successful. There are many such projects that fail on one or more of the many assessment dimensions we are covering in this book.

Call center optimization

There are so many great AI methods and tools available to aid businesses. I have been motivated and appreciative of the opportunities to think creatively to solve such problems. I had a good friend at Texas Instruments (TI), the manager of our international call center for notebook computers. I learned a great deal about call center operations from Mark, and I hope he learned some statistics and data-related ideas from me. One specific problem we worked on was call center staffing for his department.

Mark had many operational objectives, many of which were directionally opposed. He needed to keep customers happy with his agents quickly picking up the phone and addressing customer concerns. However, he was also charged with keeping costs down and not having agents sitting idly by the phone. He asked if I could help. I asked about the data available. The response was, "We have great data with any statistics you can imagine." That was great news.

There were many ways we could approach the problem with AI modeling. There were also different aims we could attempt to achieve. I wanted to be very specific about our objective. *Vague aims and objectives are one of the biggest problems in organizations today.* Everyone thinks they are speaking the same language and have the same goal, but unless you can specifically, very specifically and outline your measures and constraints, you are likely to come up short. We determined our initial objective would be median call waiting time. We had definitions for everything we measured and wanted to achieve.

We selected a queuing simulation model. Many modeling options were available, but I selected to use a statistical probabilistic model. Sounds complicated, but not too much. We had all the data so we could simulate the call center for various loads and staffing scenarios—geographic location, weekday, time of day, and special factors, and then run models across the distributions. We came up with not only a current model that would determine staffing levels by shift to **accommodate quality and minimize budget,** but we could also do scenarios such as reducing call wait time by 15 seconds. What would be the staffing personnel and financial impact?

AI technology assessment for your organization

The following steps are laid out as individual meetings, but you may break these into as many meetings as you see fit. You should plan multiple meetings. The steps are laid out first. Then, the questionnaire and worksheets are provided.

1. Team selection

As mentioned previously, your team may be uniquely selected for this assessment or contain some of the same members from other assessments. A best practice is to assign a project manager that will be part of each team to provide consistency and continuity.

2. Team education

The goal of this meeting is to educate your team on the AI readiness assessment (ARA) process. Some of the items to discuss

- The overall ARA process
- Information from this chapter

- The five projects being evaluated
- Questions and Open Discussion
- Goals and Agenda for the Next Meeting

NOTE: It is important to use the original numbering scheme for your AI initiatives/projects. These need to be consistent throughout the process. Additionally, you should have summaries of each project, including the functional departments and some of the key members contributing to the project for every initiative.

---

3. Brainstorming and open exchange

This meeting aims to educate your team on the AI readiness assessment (ARA) process. Some of the items to discuss

- Review and Opening Questions and Open Review Discussion
- AI Technology Capabilities Questionnaire
- Questions and Final Thoughts
- Goals and Agenda for the Next Meeting

NOTE: Some organizations meet to discuss the questionnaire and then assign it as homework to be reviewed as a team.

An assessment tool is offered in the following section, "AI Technology Assessment Questionnaire–

4. Scoring assessment and gap identification

This meeting aims to use the AI Technology Readiness mapping tool to rate the organizations' ability to execute AI projects. Additionally, to identify potential failure points and gaps for each project. Meeting agenda:

- Open Review of Last Meeting Notes and Questions
- Complete the AI Technology Readiness Assessment Mapping Tool
- Strengths and Weakness / Potential Failure Point Identification for each Project

An example of a Readiness Mapping Tool template is in the following section, "AI Technology Assessment Scoring."

5. Share findings with oversight committee for aggregation

Instead of a meeting, this is simply turning over the relevant materials to the oversight committee. This committee will be aggregating all functional parts of the ARA.

Questions for discussion

Gather your assessment team and any members of the leadership team and go through the following questions. Record the results.

AI technology as a strategic asset

Has your organization had any AI projects? These are any form of AI mentioned in this chapter. Were any of these projects successful? What were the (AI technology) factors that contributed to the success of these projects? Were any of these projects unsuccessful? What were the (AI technology) factors that contributed to the failure of these projects?

Is your organization AI driven? Do you make decisions based on AI applications? Do people come into meetings and support their position with material gathered from an AI platform?

Do you have leaders or managers who are actively trying to get the organization to adopt AI technology? Would you say you have AI champions?

How do you compare to your competition in the use of AI technology?

What are the biggest holdbacks for you to use AI technology more broadly?

Investment made in AI technology

Does your organization have a technology budget set aside for AI platforms? Automating actions or improving decision making? Or is it lumped into a broader budget?

Would you say your AI-related technology expenditures are rising, falling, or staying flat over time?

Do you feel it is a sufficient investment?

Are you investing in newer technology like cloud technology or services?

Are you purchasing or using marketplace ML (machine learning) models? Are you using technology like AutoML?

What percent of your AI or analytics related personnel are hired versus contracted?

Investment made on human support of AI technology

Do you have designated people whose sole job is dedicated to the creation of AI modeling or related activities? For example, data scientists, AI engineers, business analysts, and BI analysts.

Do you hire consultants or contract employees to work on AI-related technology and initiatives?

Would you say your data-related employee or consultant expenditures are rising, falling, or staying flat over time?

Do you feel it is a sufficient investment? Are you planning on hiring or contracting more help in the next few years? What about your competition, are they spending more?

Do your AI personnel fall under IT control or the business side of the house?

AI tool availability to personnel

Do you have a centralized AI platform where people across the organization can access it?

Do you have a BI (data visualization) platform accessible by people across the organization?

What technology does your organization have to improve corporate efficiency? What technology does your organization have to improve corporate decision making?

Do you have a cloud-based AI platform where people can access their data and create ML or AI models?

Are you using any mobile AI technology on phones or tablets?

Do your people believe they have the appropriate AI technology available when they need it?

Do you have self-service analytics or AI tools?

Are your AI tools primarily for your staff or external parties like consultants and contractors?

Scoring AI technology - assessment and gap identification

In this step of the assessment, you will have an open discussion with your team and come up with your capability rating for the five projects you have selected in Chapter 3, "Business Goals and Initiatives."

Please see Chapter 4, "Leadership Assessment" for a detailed example of the process. You will replicate this process for assessing the strengths and weaknesses of your AI technology toward AI project success.

Figure 15 shows a blank template for you to use. Your five business goals appear down the left side. Across the top are four areas of AI technology competency. You will fill in the 20 cells with a rating from 1 to 10 , with the lowest rating being a 1, which means you are not at all capable with this competency for this initiative up to a high rating of 10, which means you are fully capable and have no barriers or gaps in this competency to complete the initiative. You will provide a copy of your completed mapping results to the oversight committee.

Example
Business Goals

1 Reduce Manufacturing cost by 5%
2 Cut expense statement processing time to less than 5 days with 95% accuracy
3 Improve Customer Retention by 7%
4 Reduce customer service call times by 10%
5 Improve Customer Satisfaction Score by 6 points

Business Goal	AI Technology as a Strategic Asset	Investment Made in AI Technology	Investment Made on Human Support of AI Technology	AI Tool Availability to Personnel
1				
2				
3				
4				
5				

Figure 15: Scoring AI Technology Competency— Readiness Mapping Tool Template

Identification of strengths and weakness / potential failure points

The last part of the assessment to send to the oversight committee will be a list of strengths and weaknesses that can impact the likelihood of success for the initiative. We outlined a detailed example of this exercise in Chapter 4. You should identify your key strengths and weaknesses for success with each of the five projects.

Next, we aggregate the seven assessments that have been completed.

SECTION III—Project Selection, Remediation, and Kickoff

ELEVEN

Assignments Aggregated and Analyzed

> *"We are not preparing for the world we live in–- we are preparing for the world we find ourselves in."*
>
> *Michael Mabee*

Congratulations! You have accomplished a major portion of the assessment process. Now, we have to do some administrative work to see where you stand.

As discussed in Chapter 2, "An Overview of the Assessment Process," we are ready to aggregate the results. Now that all the assessment elements have been collected, we can combine them for a final view of the organizational state of readiness for its AI-powered business initiatives. We will rank the five projects proposed in Chapter 3, "Business Goals and Initiatives," and discuss the strengths and weaknesses we identified for each project.

This analysis will provide your organization with an understanding of your strengths and the initiatives you are most prepared to undertake. It will provide visibility into your readiness gaps and commentary on how you can use that information to improve your organization's readiness for the near and long term. Furthermore, it can be beneficial in annual strategic planning and budgeting processes.

In Chapter 2, we went over the eight major steps—see Figure 16. We have been through 5 of them, and it is time to step up to #6 Assignments Aggregated and Analyzed.

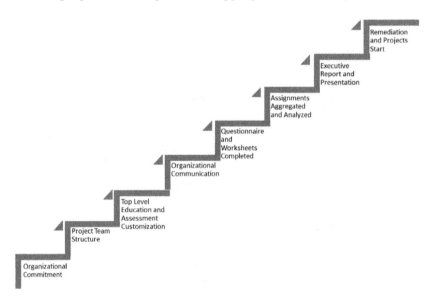

Figure 16: Simplified Business Readiness Assessment in Eight Steps

We will go through a fictional aggregation for the mapping tool and summarize the assessment results so you can see how it is done. All of the assessment teams have turned in their material to the oversight committee. Now, it is up to the committee to summarize all this material.

Figure 17: Team Structure for Assessments–Seven Assessment Teams

---

Example aggregation of mapping tools

In this section, we go through an example of aggregating the mapping tools completed from Chapter 4 through Chapter 10. We will use the same templates for each chapter but have added some hypothetical entries.

There are many ways to aggregate the data. For example, you can aggregate:

- Weighing certain dimensions higher–people, culture, etc., In the following example, we do not weigh dimensions differently. We treat every dimension as equal.

- Weighing for the number of categories. We had different numbers of categories in the mapping tool. For leadership, culture, and some others, we had four categories. For Operations and Structure, we had only three categories. For Industry and Market, we had only 2. You may decide to weigh these differently. In the following example, we weigh everything the same.

- For project selection, you can use scores or counts. In the following example, we use counts.

It is important that each assessment team use the same template structure and provide their scoring to the oversight committee. The committee can determine how the seven dimensions should be weighed.

Figure 18 is repeated from Chapter 4. This is the leadership example scoring. I have added two columns. An **Aggregate Score** and at **Top Three** designation. We can see the top AI projects. The projects the company is best prepared to successfully complete are #3, #4, and #5. The descriptions are on top of the mapping tool.

Figure 19 is an example of culture assessment scoring. We can see that the top AI projects, which the company is best prepared to successfully complete, are #2, #3, and #5.

Example - Leadership
Business Goals
    1 Reduce Manufacturing cost by 5%
    2 Cut expense statement processing time to less than 5 days with 95% accuracy
    3 Improve Customer Retention by 7%
    4 Reduce customer service call times by 10%
    5 Improve Customer Satisfaction Score by 6 points

Business Goal	Trust and Positive Relations	Willingness to Take Chances and Not Blame Failures, Reward Learning	Alignment and Collaboration	Commitment	Aggregate Score	Top 3
1	6	6	6	7	25	
2	7	8	8	6	29	
3	8	9	9	10	36	X
4	8	8	9	6	31	X
5	8	9	9	10	36	X

Figure 18: Evaluation Scores for Leadership with our 5 Business Goals

Business Goal	Adaptable and innovative	Continual learning and improvement	Strong team Focus and member maturity	Willingness to risk failure	Aggregate Score	Top 3
1	5	6	5	7	23	
2	7	8	8	7	30	X
3	8	7	7	10	32	X
4	9	7	7	5	28	
5	8	9	9	10	36	X

Figure 19: Evaluation Scores for Culture

Figure 20 is an example of operations and structure assessment scoring. We can see that the top AI projects that are best prepared to successfully complete are #1, #2, and #3.

Business Goal	Functions, Roles and Hierarchy Access	Ability to Adapt/Change for Creativity and Human Capital	Organizational Resiliency		Aggregate Score	Top 3
1	9	8	8		25	X
2	8	7	5		20	X
3	7	7	7		21	X
4	4	6	6		16	
5	5	7	5		17	

Figure 20: Evaluation Scores for Operations and Structure

Figure 21 is an example of industry and market assessment scoring. We can see that the top AI projects (the projects the company is best prepared to successfully complete), are also #1, #2, and #3.

Business Goal	Ability to Respond to Market Changes	Ability to Respond to Industry Changes	Aggregate Score	Top 3
1	8	9	17	X
2	8	8	16	X
3	7	8	15	X
4	6	7	13	
5	7	5	12	

Figure 21: Evaluation Scores for Industry and Market

Figure 22 is an example of people assessment scoring. We can see that the top AI projects are #1, #3, and #5.

Business Goal	Skills and Knowledge	Aptitude / Willingness to Learn	Open Mindedness and Emotional Intelligence	Drive and Attitude to Succeed	Aggregate Score	Top 3
1	10	9	7	9	35	X
2	7	6	6	6	25	
3	8	9	9	10	36	X
4	7	7	6	5	25	
5	9	8	10	9	36	X

Figure 22: Evaluation Scores for People

Figure 23 is an example of data assessment scoring. We can see that the top AI projects, that is, the projects the company is best prepared to successfully complete, are #1, #4, and #5.

Business Goal	Data as a Strategic Asset	Investment Made in Data	Data Quality and Consistency	Data Availability	Aggregate Score	Top 3
1	10	10	8	8	36	X
2	7	6	6	6	25	
3	5	6	6	6	23	
4	10	8	8	8	34	X
5	7	8	7	7	29	X

Figure 23: Evaluation Scores for Data

Figure 24 is an example of AI technology assessment scoring. We can see that the top AI projects are also #1, #4, and #5.

Business Goal	AI Technology as a Strategic Asset	Investment Made in AI Technology	Investment Made on Human Support of AI Technology	AI Tool Availability to Personnel	Aggregate Score	Top 3
1	7	7	8	8	30	X
2	5	5	5	5	20	
3	5	5	6	5	21	
4	7	7	7	8	29	X
5	6	5	6	5	22	X

Figure 24: Evaluation Scores for AI Technology

We want to select the top three AI projects to initiate for this simple example. So, we use counts to determine which AI projects the organization is best prepared to execute successfully. In Figure 25, we have a list of the seven dimensions relating to success across the top row and business goals listed down the side. We check the cells that make the top three from the previous numerical ranking for each dimension. Finally, we add a simple count of the checks for projects that make the top 3. Projects 1, 3, and 5 are most likely to succeed across the assessment dimensions.

Business Goals	Leadership Capable	Culture Capable	Operations and Structure Capable	Industry and Market Capable	People Capable	Data Capable	AI Technology Capable	Count
1		X		X	X	X	X	5
2	X	X		X				3
3	X	X	X	X	X			5
4	X					X	X	3
5	X	X			X	X	X	5

Figure 25: Vote Tallies Across the 7 Critical Dimensions

We have now completed the quantitative part of the assessment and the following are the project selections to move forward to the next step.

- Reduce manufacturing cost by 5%.

- Improve customer retention by 7%.
- Improve customer satisfaction score by 6 points.

Strengths and weakness / potential failure points

The oversight committee can decide how it would like to receive information on each assessment team's strengths and weaknesses. It may be a structured format that everyone uses, or it could be more freeform. Each has its advantages. One idea is to provide the top three contributors to success and the top three antagonists against success for all proposed business initiatives. For example, we chose to do this for only two of the five AI projects in Chapter 4.

We provided these examples of strengths and weaknesses in Chapter 4 when we evaluated leadership's readiness assessment. We provided some overall commentary and then we selected two examples to illustrate what the process looked like. An example that scored lower than most is "#1 Reduce Manufacturing cost by 5% ." And another example that scored higher than most is "#3 Improve Customer Retention by 7% ." In reality, the assessment team would describe all five in the document they share with the oversight committee.

Please review those two examples. They should serve as informative examples. We will not carry this out for every dimension–it would be voluminous and of limited value. However, *the information contained in this descriptive material is very important.* It captures details of where your organization is strong and ready to take on a specific AI project. More importantly, it outlines what gaps must be addressed to prepare the organization for this specific AI project.

The oversight committee will now take this information to create an executive report and presentation for senior leadership. We will cover that in the following chapter.

TWELVE

Executive Report and Presentation

You have accomplished a great deal and now is the time to share your findings with senior leadership! It is time for your teams to shine by creating reports and presentations, and then deliver and discuss valuable insights with executives. This is step 7 of our 8-step business readiness assessment process illustrated in Figure 26.

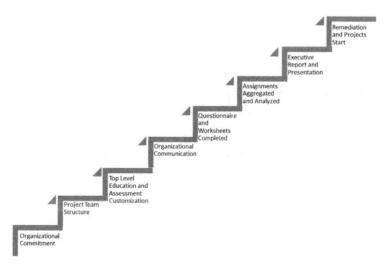

Figure 26: Simplified Business Readiness Assessment in Eight Steps

Report and presentation team

Once all the assignments have been aggregated and analyzed, the project manager or leader of the oversight committee will assemble a small team to put together an executive report for senior leadership. This team will complete the following.

- A report with the AI readiness assessment findings.
- Prepare an executive presentation.
- Deliver the executive presentation and report.

Note: Why a small team? In my experience, having the entire committee compile the report and presentation lacks efficiency. So, a subgroup of the committee is preferred if the committee is large.

1. ARA report creation

One of the key activities we noted throughout the book was the importance of having good scribe notes and team documentation of the process. Relevant documentation greatly facilitates report creation. You may have a corporate template or method of creating reports. My experience suggests three recommendations:

- Be Terse and Direct
- Be Honest
- Be Positive

You will customize your report for your situation, but it should include:

- The importance of the ARA process to the future of the business.
- Recognition of the keep contributors and participants.
- Findings of the process.
- Initiatives considered and recommendations to move forward.
- Team composition for every recommended initiative. Any funding needs and remediation efforts.
- Corporate commitment to AI initiatives moving forward.

2. ARA presentation preparation

Some companies present their findings by going through the written report. The better option is to create a short slide deck and present the highlights during the formal meeting. Wait to hand over the written report at the end of the meeting. Here are the advantages:

- You do not want participants rifling through pages. It is distracting.
- You want to guide the conversation.
- You want to filter the information to the key points.
- You want leadership to focus on what you want them to focus on

- You want leadership to endorse your recommendations.
- You want leaders to commit to a future presentation of results after project completion.
- After project completion and conditioned upon successful results, you want a commitment to budget, expand AI projects, and potentially form an AI program.

So, your slides will cover the key points of the ARA process, your findings, and a call for endorsement. *The deck should be very short!* Your objective is an open discussion and the endorsement from leaders to move forward.

---

3. ARA presentation meeting

Finally, after preparing the formal report and your slide deck, you will schedule a meeting with senior leadership to review the results. Recommendations:

- Again, I would keep slides to a bare minimum, focused on key things to cover.
- Keep on Track. Allow for discussion, but do not let it take you off focus. You want commitments made.
- You need to be well prepared. You need the presenters' roles and responsibilities assigned and you should practice your presentation. It needs to be crisp and to the point.

- Leave time at the end and ask for approval. If decision makers need more time, have them commit to a date in the near term.

NOTE: If you keep leadership well informed through the process, it greatly improves the odds of getting a quick endorsement.

After leadership has committed and plans finalized, we need to make a formal communication with the entire organization. It will outline:

- The importance of the project to the future of the business.
- Recognition of the key contributors and participants.
- Findings of the project.
- Initiatives being started as a result of the project.
- Corporate commitment to AI initiatives moving forward.

In the next chapter, we will discuss bridging gaps and kicking off your initiatives.

THIRTEEN

Remediation and Projects Start

You have made a great presentation to senior leadership. You have expressed the importance of AI and data-based decision making. You have shared the AI threat from your competition and the consequences of inaction. You have advanced recommendations for the top AI-powered initiatives the organization should undertake. You expressed needs required, funding, and remediation efforts. Leadership has endorsed these projects. Now, it is time for that work to begin. This is the final step of our 8-step business readiness assessment step process illustrated in Figure 27.

Next steps

You should form teams and work on individual AI projects now that you have full leadership support. The oversight committee will form AI initiative work groups. That is, AI implementation teams to carry the projects forward. Each initiative, however many you choose, will have an implementation team. Your organization may want to form an overarching AI committee or AI program office in the future. More on that in the following section, Future State.

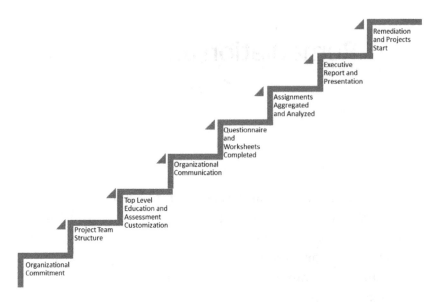

Figure 27: Simplified Business Readiness Assessment in Eight Steps

Team selection is very important. You have a head start based on the assessment process as we noted in Step 2 of each assessment dimension that, "You should have summaries of each project including the functional departments and some of the key members contributing to the project." You will determine the appropriate next steps. However, here are three suggested steps and recommendations.

Three major steps with recommendations

1. Capitalize on your *strengths*.

   a. Use your strengths to your advantage, especially on the human capital side. Make sure you enlist people who will make your initiatives a success.

   b. Make necessary schedule changes to allow designated internal personnel time away from their routine schedule to participate.

   c. Remind leadership of their commitment, often. Share any intermediate results. Stay honest, positive, and directed.

2. Fill in any gaps or *weaknesses*.

   a. Any known budget needs necessary should have been addressed in the senior level presentation covered in the last chapter. If any remain, rectify immediately.

   b. If you need to acquire any help from the outside, do so. However, you should always have a plan in place to bolster your internal knowledge from these outside participants. This means that every dollar paid to the outside has double the benefit.

   c. Any applicable investments that require internal education should be made.

    d. Any applicable restructuring or personnel incentives should be made.

    e. Any applicable investments in data or AI should be made.

3. *Start* the Projects!

    a. If you do not have a formal kickoff process, start one. There should be some fanfare and everyone within the organization should know that senior leadership has endorsed these initiatives. Get the troops motivated!

    b. Produce an update cadence. You need frequent reports and occasional meetings between the AI implementation teams and the oversight committee.

    c. At a minimum, you should have quarterly updates from senior leadership, the oversight committee, and implementation teams. With the right planning, this can be minimally invasive and very beneficial.

Future state

A project by definition is of a limited time frame. If successful, it becomes a sustainable process. Hopefully, most of the AI-driven initiatives you have undertaken become corporate processes.

Importantly, you have shared the success of this first iteration of the process with senior leadership and they see the value. There are two future states if so:

1. Start a second iteration of the ARA process again with new business initiatives.

2. Turn the process nature of the oversight committee into a full program. That is, an AI program committee or AI program office. This is an ongoing sustainable structure.

We close the last chapter with a few parting thoughts to improve your process over time.

FOURTEEN

Parting Thoughts

We have covered a lot of material. You have a firm foundation on what matters most to the success of AI projects. Now, you just need to customize it for your unique situation.

We have covered one iteration. Your first pass will be a bit daunting, but you will learn from each iteration, and it will get easier and easier as you move forward. We have noted that not every project will succeed, but if you succeed in more than half of your projects, you will beat the average and gain significant ROI. We also noted that those who do not change their business model will not survive the new AI age. It is not a novelty. It is a necessity.

As you move through your AI program journey, you will have project successes and shortcomings. You need to continually evaluate your progress and learn from the process.

First, you should always assess the degree of success with a project. You need to conduct post-activity reviews. Second, you must think critically about your decision-making before deciding which projects to take on.

Too often, in corporate and personal decisions, we simply want to replicate decisions that led to success and avoid decisions that came up short. That is not the proper way to learn and evolve. Here are some tips for future iterations:

- **Document every success and every shortfall.** Understand why you are lacking and why you are succeeding. A post-project business review is essential.

- **Keep it as simple as possible.** Einstein said, "Everything should be made as simple as possible, but not simpler."

- **Learn from your decision process, not your outcomes.** Do not analyze a project outcome based solely on whether it was a successful project or if it came up short. Some things contribute to outcomes that are beyond your control. A good poker player does not evaluate their game based on whether they won or lost. They evaluate what they were thinking at the time that led to their decision and the actions taken. *Improving the way you think and learn is within your control.*

Let me know how your process is going. Please contact me at:

ItsAllAnalytics.com

Wishing you the best of success!

Scott

Index